Myth of Foreign Terrorism

The events of 9/11 were not acts of foreign terrorism

Hans Sherrer

The Justice Institute (Seattle)

Published by:
The Justice Institute
PO Box 66291
Seattle, WA 98166
www.justicedenied.org
info@justicedenied.org

First print edition, September 2018

Trade Paperback ISBN: 1727597389
Trade Paperback ISBN-13: 978-1727597387

Front and Back cover photographs from top to bottom credited to: metro.co.uk; rainbowwarrior2005.wordpress.com; and 911review.com.

Printed in the U.S.A.
This book is printed on acid free paper

Table of Contents

Foreword

The *Myth Of Foreign Terrorism* was published in December 2002 on the forejustice.org Internet website.[1] Over the last 16 years many tens of thousands of copies have been downloaded.

In 2002 the world of book publishing was much different than today. The *Myth Of Foreign Terrorism* would have been formally published at that time if today's options of reasonable self-publishing had been available at that time.

When it was written and published online in 2002 there were only a few books and websites devoted to exploring inconsistencies in the official version of 9/11, and the U.S. had not yet invaded Iraq. After recently reading The *Myth Of Foreign Terrorism* for the first time in many years, I realized that events of the last sixteen years have validated the three basic themes of the book, and that a truly amazing amount of research now supports that the federal government's official version of 9/11 is even more disconnected from reality than it appeared to be based on the information available in 2002 – only a year after 9/11.

Consequently, I decided to rectify that it wasn't published in hardcopy as a book in 2002, by doing so belatedly, and ensure that it will be available regardless of what happens to its availability on the Internet.

The following chapters have been added related to particularly important information learned since 2002:

1. Osama bin Laden was never indicted for 9/11, and he never publicly stated he and/or Al-Qaeda was involved.

2. Seventeen years after 9/11 no one has credibly taken credit for it.

3. Malaysian Airline flight FH370 disappeared on March 8, 2014 and its wreckage has not been found in the Indian Ocean.

4. The War on Terror was triggered by 9/11 events that remain mysterious.

5. The U.S. military invaded Iraq in 2003, following its invasion of Afghanistan in 2001, and it is still active in those, and other middle-eastern countries as part of the United State's never ending "war on terror."

6. The liberty of Americans has been under assault since Sept. 11, 2001.

Hans Sherrer
September 2018

---

[1] Hans Sherrer, *The Myth of Foreign Terrorism*, 2002. Online at, http://forejustice.org/write/myth_of_terrorism.pdf .

Introduction

(December 2002)

There are three intertwining themes to this book. The central theme underlying the other two is that the events involving four diverted airliners in the eastern United States on the morning of September 11, 2001 were not acts of foreign terrorism. This book details there is no definitional basis to even suggest, much less substantiate that those events were foreign terrorism. That fact is an antidote to the steady stream of news stories, magazine articles, books, media programs, editorials and op-ed pieces, and political speeches that have combined to imprint the idea in the mind of many people they were foreign terrorism.

The mistaken belief that September 11th involved foreign terrorism has become so pervasive that it qualifies as a form of urban legend. It is an idea that has been widely accepted without proof. There have been so many loose references to foreign terrorism since September 11th, that clearing away the semantic fog that has generated false public perceptions about those events reveals the plain truth that the terrorism against Americans related to September 11th wasn't perpetrated by foreigners.

The book's second theme, with all it suggests and entails, is that in stark contrast to the absence of foreign terrorism, a systematic and very public campaign of domestic terrorism against Americans by the President and his Cabinet, members of Congress, and officials of multiple federal agencies was begun soon after the World Trade Center buildings were struck. That terrorist campaign is disconcerting in the absence of any other consideration. However, it is compounded by the suspicious circumstances of what occurred prior to, on, and after September 11, the scale of the operation necessary to orchestrate those events, that no organization or group has taken credit for them, and that the federal government and those associated with it are not just the most conspicuous beneficiaries of those events, but they are the *only* visible direct beneficiaries of them. Thus the factors of means, motive, opportunity, magnitude, and who benefited from September 11th all point to those events were acts of domestic terrorism.[2]

However, one need look no further than that the events of September 11th were not acts of foreign terrorism to understand the federal legislation and the United States' attack on Afghanistan justified as a response to those events, were respectively enacted and launched under false pretenses. Which means what is described as the federal government's "War on Terrorism" is a sham.

Why? Because the only terrorism the American people have been, and are being subjected to is being perpetrated against them by the federal government in the form of such things as the Patriot Act of 2001, the Homeland Security Act of 2002, the federalization of airport screeners, the Defense Department's Information Assurance Office, and the incessant drumbeat by politicians and their supporters in the media that we must fear the foreign terrorists hell-bent on harming the United States. Furthermore, widespread public and media support for those responses is attributable to the trigger events of September 11.

The book's third theme is the threat to the liberty of Americans by people, agencies and organizations within the United States – directly or indirectly associated with the federal government – that are seeking emasculation of the Bill of Rights. Such an agenda can only be accomplished by people with access to the inner sanctum of power in Washington D.C., and not by politically impotent foreigners outside the country who can do nothing to undermine the liberty of Americans. It is only political insiders or people and organizations with meaningful access to them, that can obliterate the liberty of Americans by unleashing the Constitution from the Bill of Rights' symbolic constraint against the unfettered use of its powers against individual men, women and children.

So quite contrary to the assertion of many analysts of the fall-out from the events of September 11th, the campaign in their wake has been to exalt the federal government's powers under the Constitution as supreme over the shield of protections afforded individuals and their associations under the Bill of Rights. Thus it isn't the Constitution that is hated – but the Bill of Rights – just as it was in 1787 by the "founding fathers."

In summary, the three themes of this book are:

First, the events of September 11, 2001 involving four diverted commercial airliners were not acts of foreign terrorism

Second, in the wake of the events of September 11, 2001, systematic terrorism campaigns were begun by the federal government and those associated with it against American's domestically, and against Afghanistan, and other countries internationally.

Third, the liberty of Americans is being assaulted by identifiable efforts to divest the Bill of Rights' shield of actual and symbolic protection from unfettered application of the Constitution against men, women and children in this country, both individually and collectively.

---

[2] As the text will make clear, it is certainly within the realm of possibility that the events of September 11, 2001 involved at least indirectly, and very possibly directly, people within, and associated with the federal government.

I

The Bastardization of Words For Political Advantage

Although most well known for his prophetic 1949 novel, *Nineteen Eighty-Four*, George Orwell was a renowned social and political essayist in the 1930s and 40s. Many of the ideas in his novel about the use of language to politically control people are a refinement of what he wrote about in his 1945 essay: *Politics and the English Language*.[3] That essay explains among other things, the crucial role of words in galvanizing support by the general population for and against a particular political cause or action. Orwell explained that clouding the meaning of words is an important element of that process, because slovenly use "of our language makes it easier for us to have foolish thoughts."[4] Since we concretize thoughts in terms of words, any corruption of the language one uses inevitably leads to a corruption in the expression of one's thoughts and actions related to those thoughts.

So those who influence the use of a language can manipulate the images created in the minds of people that they transpose for reality. Thus an enduring cultural contribution of George Orwell's essay was clarifying how bastardization of a language's use is essential to publicly mask the reality of political events and rallying support for rationally unsupportable policies. Orwell explained this process in a passage of *Politics and the English Language* that is as important in its implications as any written in the 20th Century:

"In our time, political speech and writing are largely the defense of the indefensible. Things like the continuance of British rule in India, the Russian purges and deportations, the [Americans] dropping of the atom bombs on Japan, can indeed be defended, but only by arguments which are too brutal for most people to face, and which do not square with the professed aims of the political parties. Thus political language has to consist largely of euphemism, question-begging and sheer cloudy vagueness. Defenseless villages are bombarded from the air, the inhabitants driven out into the countryside, the cattle machine-gunned, the huts set on fire with incendiary bullets: this is called *pacification*. Millions of peasants are robbed of their farms and sent trudging along the roads with no more than they can carry: this is called transfer of *population or rectification of frontiers*. People are imprisoned for years without trial, or shot in the back of the neck or sent to die of scurvy in Arctic lumber camps: this is called *elimination of unreliable elements*. Such phraseology is needed if one wants to name things without calling up mental pictures of them. Consider for instance some comfortable English professor defending Russian totalitarianism. He cannot say outright, "I believe in killing off your opponents when you can get good results by doing so." Probably, therefore, he will say something like this:

> "While freely conceding that the Soviet regime exhibits certain features which the humanitarian may be inclined to deplore, we must, I think, agree that a certain curtailment of the right to political opposition is an unavoidable concomitant of transitional periods, and that the rigors which the Russian people have been called upon to undergo have been amply justified in the sphere of concrete achievement."

The inflated style itself is a kind of euphemism. A mass of Latin words falls upon the facts like soft snow, blurring the outline and covering up all the details. The great enemy of clear language is insincerity. When there is a gap between one's real and one's declared aims, one turns as it were instinctively to long words and exhausted idioms, like a cuttlefish spurting out ink. In our age there is no such thing as "keeping out of politics." All issues are political issues, and politics itself is a mass of lies, evasions, folly, hatred, and schizophrenia."[5]

The relevance of Orwell's observations about the use of language as a tool of political obfuscation is greater today than in his day. The sphere of political influence in daily life is infinitely greater than in 1945 when Orwell wrote his essay, and the use of language as a tool to muddle the perception people have about events with political implications has grown apace.

Linguistic concealment of political actions and motives is the single greatest threat to the people of any society, because they permit the imposition and continuation of policies that would be laid bare for what they are if words were used that accurately described the policies, and/or the events that may have precipitated their enactment. This is true regardless of a countries political structure or language, since as Orwell notes, language bastardization is prevalent in countries of different political persuasions.[6]

When it comes to the bastardization of words for political advantage, the U.S. doesn't take a backseat to any country. That is amply demonstrated by the false description of the events of September 11, 2001 as foreign terrorism.

---

[3] *Politics and the English Language*, George Orwell, *The Collected Essays, Journalism and Letters of George Orwell*, edited by Sonia Orwell and Ian George, Harcourt Brace Jovanovich, New York, 1968. This essay was written in May 1945, the month Germany surrendered ending the war in Europe.

[4] *Id.*

[5] *Id.*

[6] *Id.*

The Bastardization of Words For Political Advantage

II
Words in English Have Known Definitions

The key to understanding the events of September 11th weren't acts of terrorism is that a feature of the English language is all words have one or more specific and identifiable meanings. Those meanings relate to other words or phrases that describe what is meant by use of the word. A word's primary and secondary definitions help facilitate meaningful communication by enabling the concepts and ideas contained in the definition to be transmitted by use of the word alone.

So a word can accurately be characterized as a shorthand expression for what is represented by its definition. When one word proves inadequate to convey the meaning of a thought, it is common for two words to be combined by a hyphen to make a more expressive word. It is also possible for entirely new words to be created for expressing a concept or idea in a new or unique way.

The adaptability of English by the free-flow combining of existing or addition of new words is one way that English retains its vibrancy and relevance in a changing world.

There is consequently no need to risk confusing people by summarily and unilaterally altering or changing the definition of an existing word to express a new thought or idea: since English imposes no impediment to the instant creation of a new word that will have a definition accurately expressing that thought or idea.

The free-flowing nature of English is exhibited by its heritage. When Shakespeare was writing his plays there was no comprehensive English dictionary. His audience would understand his use of English due to their educational backgrounds and geographical proximity to him.

As the mobility of people and the geographical audience of what was written increased, the need for people in different areas or educational backgrounds to comprehend the use of words in a mutually understandable manner also increased. That need to communicate clearly contributed to the creation of the dictionary as a method of linking a word with its meaning(s) and forms of use.

The most complete of the early dictionaries was Samuel Johnson's, first published in 1755.[7] It remained the most comprehensive dictionary of the English language until the first installment of the Oxford English Dictionary was made available to the public over 100 years later.

The value of dictionaries to facilitate understanding has been proven during the past 250 years. The reliance on dictionaries to document a word's meaning has become so universal that today there are a multitude of general and specialized dictionaries. Some words have technical and non-technical definitions. Medical terms for example, are specifically defined in a medical dictionary, and they may or may not be generally defined in lay person terms in a popular dictionary.

Legal terms are the same. Many words commonly used in newspapers, magazines, books, on television and in daily conversation – such as guilt, innocence, custody and assault – are legally defined. However, common use doesn't affect a word's legal meaning, which may be consistent with the lay meaning.

Some legal terms that have lay person meanings are also statutorily defined by a legislative enactment.

There are also words with *general*, *legal* and *statutory* connotations that are ascribed a definition by *law enforcement* agencies. Terrorism is one such word.

---

[7] *The Dictionary of the English Language* by Jack Lynch. Available at: http://newark.rutgers.edu/~jlynch/Johnson/Guide/dict.html . Samuel Johnson wrote the definitions of over 40,000 words, illustrating them with about 114,000 quotations drawn from every field of learning. See the biography of Samuel Johnson at: http://www.kirjasto.sci.fi/samuelj.htm.

III

How Was Terrorism Defined On September 11, 2001?

Terrorism is an over 200 year-old word that is specifically defined. On September 11, 2001 it was defined *generally, legally, statutorily* and by *law enforcement* agencies.

The best selling dictionary of any kind in the United States is *Merriam-Webster's Collegiate Dictionary*. The tenth edition *generally* defines terrorism as: "the systematic use of terror esp. as a means of coercion."[8] That meaning directly links to that dictionary's definition of terror: "violence (as bombing) committed by groups in order to intimidate a population or government into granting their demands."[9]

The most widely used legal dictionary in the United States is *Black's Law Dictionary*. The seventh edition *legally* defines terrorism as: "The use or threat of violence to intimidate or cause panic, esp. as a means of affecting political conduct. – terrorist."[10]

Since 1983 the U.S. government has relied on the statutory definition of terrorism in 22 United States Code §2656(f)(d)(2) for statistical and analytical purposes. That *statutory* definition is: "the term "terrorism" means premeditated, politically motivated violence perpetrated against noncombatant targets by subnational groups or clandestine agents [usually intended to influence an audience.]"[11]

Furthermore, the FBI's *law enforcement* definition of terrorism has remained unchanged for years: "…terrorism is the unlawful use of force or violence against persons or property to intimidate or coerce a government, the civilian population, or any segment thereof, in furtherance of political or social objectives."[12]

Those four definitions reflect a common understanding that there are two prongs that must be satisfied for an act to be classified as terrorism.

The first prong is the act *must* be intended to influence political policies ("intimidate a … government into granting their demands," *Merriam-Webster's Collegiate Dictionary*; "affecting political conduct," *Black's Law Dictionary*; "politically motivated violence," 22 U.S.C. §2656(f)(d)(2); and, "in furtherance of political … objectives," F.B.I.'s definition).

The second prong is the act is perpetrated by one or more persons allied with an identifiable group ("committed by groups" *Merriam-Webster's*

Collegiate Dictionary; "The use or threat of violence … [by a] terrorist" *Black's Law Dictionary*; "by subnational groups or clandestine agents" 22 U.S.C. §2656f(d)(2); and, "unlawful use of force or violence" F.B.I.'s definition.).[13]

So all four classes of defining terrorism are complementary in recognizing that the two prongs that must be satisfied for an act to be considered as terrorism are it is intended to affect political policies, and it involves people associated with a group.

---

[8] *Merriam-Webster's Collegiate Dictionary*, 10th Edition, p. 1217.

[9] *Id.*

[10] *Black's Law Dictionary*, 7th Edition, p. 1484.

[11] From: *Patterns of Global Terrorism*. Washington: Dept. of State, 2001: vi, cited at: http://www.history.navy.mil/library/guides/terrorism.htm#general. This definition is used by the U.S. government to determine whether it is appropriate to classify an act of violence as terrorism. The federal government explicitly recognizes that violence, per se, is not classifiable as terrorism in the absence of the caveat that it be "politically motivated violence."

[12] "The FBI defines terrorism is the unlawful use of force or violence against persons or property to intimidate or coerce a government, the civilian population, or any segment thereof, in furtherance of political or social objectives." Terrorism in the United States: 1996, Federal Bureau of Investigation, p. 3. This same definition is the FBI's report for 1999, although it is attributed to 28 C.F.R §0.85.

[13] A couple of the definitions don't exclude the theoretical possibility that an individual can engage in terrorism. For all practical purposes, however, logistical reasons exclude an individual from being able to do so with anything other than temporary or localized effectiveness. So acts by an individual that could be labeled as terrorism are more symbolic than real.

The Unabomber is an example of a lone person that some people might try to classify as engaging in terrorism. However he wasn't. The Unabomber's actions were so inconsequential in their impact on how people acted, that regardless of their motive they can't be considered as being intended to influence political policies anymore than one can consider the shooting of a pop-gun will be effective at stopping a charging bull.

So while acts of violence by an individual may be a symbolic "blow" for some personal or philosophical cause, they are rarely acts of terrorism: such acts by an individual are not even potentially politically influential – so they don't meet terrorism's first and most important prong of being intended to affect political policy.

     How Was Terrorism Defined On September 11, 2001?

IV
What Are Acts Of Terrorism?

Some of the purest and most undisputed acts of terrorism are bombings and other acts of violence by the IRA over a more than 30-year period against civilian and military personnel and targets in Northern Ireland and England. These events have been widely reported in the news media. How is it known the IRA was involved? The IRA claimed responsibility. How is it known they were intended to influence political policies? The IRA made it plainly known the purpose of their actions was to influence the British to abandon their political policy of occupying Northern Ireland, to withdraw their troops from the country, and to accept the unimpeded political self-determination of the country. Furthermore, the IRA's claims of responsibility were credible: the violence occurred in areas and situations that would maximize publicity for their cause, and they were consistent with the sort of activity the IRA was known to be involved in.[14] The IRA openly claims responsibility for acts of violence it is involved in, and so its denial of involvement in an action is credible.

The detonating of bombs strapped to Palestinians amongst crowds of people in Israel as a political tactic is another example of self-evident terrorism. The Palestinians responsible readily take credit for the bombings that are specifically intended to influence Israel to grant their political demands. It can't be overlooked that the Palestinians are routinely setting off bombs and engaging in gunfights with Israeli troops and police, even though Israeli has draconian "anti-terrorism" legislation in effect and is run closer to the model of a total police state than any other country in the world.

There are numerous other violent acts by groups around the world that clearly fall within terrorism's spectrum of being specifically intended to influence political policy to the perpetrator's advantage.

During the Vietnam War several groups in the U.S. committed violent acts they readily took credit for that were intended to influence the federal government to end its involvement in that conflict. Those domestic groups clearly met the two primary prongs defining an act as one of terrorism: 1) an action intended to affect political policies, 2) by people associated with a group. One of those domestic terrorist organizations was the Weather Underground which engaged in bombings of government facilities. Their leaders included Bernardine Dohrn and Bill Ayers.[15] After they were captured both Dohrn and Ayers, who were married, became college professors and outspoken critics of the U.S. government and its policies.

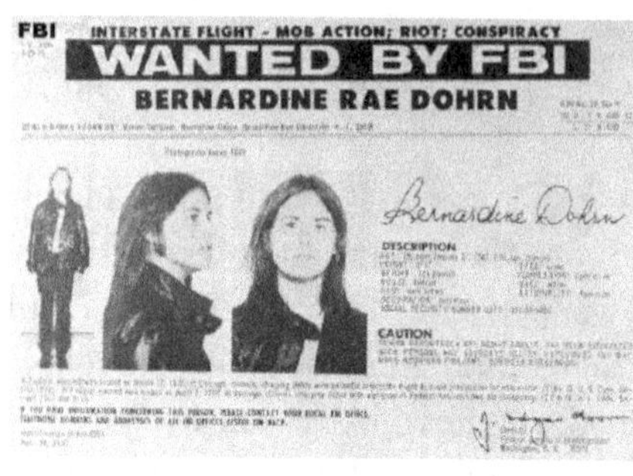

---

[14] One example is *Bloody Friday*, July 21, 1972: An Irish Republican Army (IRA) bomb attack killed 11 people and injured 130 in Belfast, Northern Ireland. Ten days later, three IRA car bomb attacks in the village of Claudy left six dead. Source: Significant Terrorist Incidents, 1961-2001, U.S. Dept. of State, Office of the Historian, Bureau of Public Affairs, October 31, 2001.

[15] *The Weather Underground* (2002) Documentary directed by Sam Green and Bill Siegel. https://www.imdb.com/title/tt0343168/ .

V

The Myth September 11th Were Acts of Foreign Terrorism

Osama bin Laden and his al-Qaeda associates have been publicly accused by high-ranking U.S. government officials of masterminding and executing the events of September 11, 2001. The news media in this country have duly and uncritically reported those accusations. However, when those events are looked at from the perspective of the *general, legal, statutory* and *law enforcement* definitions of terrorism, it is evident that neither Osama bin Laden nor anyone associated with him has been accused of an act of terrorism at any time since those events occurred. Why? Neither bin Laden nor anyone identifiable as acting under his direction has made any demands or attempted to politically influence the U.S. government or any governmental organization in *any* country related to the events of September 11th. Furthermore, neither bin Laden nor anyone allegedly acting under his direction has publicly taken credit for the events of September 11, 2001. That is consistent with the lack of anyone linked with bin Laden exerting any pressure or making any political demands on the U.S. government. That fact is also consistent with the reported inability of the U.S. government to find a link between *any* of the alleged nineteen hijackers of the four airplanes and bin Laden or al-Qaeda after more than a year of intensive investigation.[16]

Thus the public accusations against Osama bin Laden and al-Qaeda do not allege they committed or were involved in acts of terrorism. Since terrorism's first prong cannot be satisfied even if it is ever proved beyond a reasonable doubt that bin Laden and his associates were involved in the events of September 11th, their role would only have been as part of *a crime.* Consequently, they would be entitled to the procedures built into the criminal law and assured by the Bill of Rights – including the right to consult with an attorney, bail, and a speedy and public trial by a jury of lay people.

Furthermore, not only are bin Laden and *all* of his associates excluded from having been involved in an act of terrorism related to the events of September 11th, but no group of *any* political, ethnic or religious persuasion has taken credit for those events. That is reflected in the fact that *no demands* have been made of the federal government related to the events of September 11th by *any* group claiming credit for them as part of a demand to influence political policy in the U.S.

Relying individually or collectively on the four definitions of terrorism makes one fact crystal clear. Even if one were to accept argumentum that the scenario pawned off by the federal government – that nineteen allegedly foreign hijackers allegedly commandeered four airliners on September 11, 2001 – bears some relationship to the truth, those people can not be considered to have been involved in an act of foreign terrorism, much less one involving Osama bin Laden, al-Qaeda, or any other foreign NGO or government. That conclusion is self-evident by simply relying on the accepted premise that using words in a manner consistent with their definitions is essential to clearly communicating ideas and concepts.

That leads one to make the inescapable conclusion the media has been complicit in fostering the politically generated myth that the events of September 11, 2001 were acts of foreign terrorism by Osama bin Laden and al-Qaeda Islamic fundamentalists.

The events of September 11th are not the first time an illusory event has been transformed by political and media forces into an act of foreign aggression against the U.S. The media similarly acted as confederates with the federal government by reporting as a true event, the manufactured story that an American destroyer was subjected to an intense torpedo attack by North Vietnamese PT boats in the Gulf of Tonkin on August 4, 1964. An employee of the Department of Defense at the time, Daniel Ellsberg gives a first hand account in *Secrets: A Memoir of Vietnam and the Pentagon Papers* (2002), of the duplicity by military and political leaders in lying to the American people about the non-existent North Vietnamese attack.[17] Reported as if it actually happened, that fictitious attack was used to justify passage of the Gulf of Tonkin Resolution on August 7, 1964.[18] Although it was based on a non-existent provocation, that Resolution paved the way for escalation of the U.S.'s involvement in Vietnam's civil war that ultimately led to the deaths of over 50,000 American servicemen and the maiming of tens of thousands more.

Even closer to our time, the 1991 Gulf War was based on a non-existent lie perpetrated on the American people by the U.S. government. The justification for the Gulf War was the Iraqi army was alleged to have been poised for an imminent attack on Saudi Arabia. The U.S. government claimed that such an event would endanger the national interest of the U.S. by potentially affecting Saudi Arabia's supply of oil to this country. To sell the idea that Iraq was prepared to attack Saudi Arabia, the U.S. government, under the leadership of President George H.W. Bush, claimed that "classified satellite images showed that up to 250,000 Iraqi troops and 1,500 tanks had amassed on the border of Saudi Arabia."[19] At the time Saddam Hussein denied he was preparing to attack Saudi Arabia.

The *St. Petersburg Times* obtained two commercial satellite images of the area between Iraq and Saudi Arabia taken at the time the classified photos allegedly showed Iraq's army poised for an attack. The commercial photos show an empty desert.[20] The Gulf War of 1991 was based on nothing but a fabrication by the U.S. government that was perpetrated on the American people as the truth by the Bush administration and its willing dupes in the news media. As in the Vietnam conflict also created from thin air by the lies of politicians reported as the truth, hundreds of thousands of American servicemen were harmed due to the Gulf War.[21]

The federal government's manufacture of a justification out of thin air for the 1991 Gulf War was consistent with, and added another chapter to the U.S. government's rich history of bending the truth or simply creating untruths from whole cloth to publicly justify its intention to become involved in an armed conflict. Tactics of fabrication and deceit were also used by the U.S. government to involve the U.S. in the Civil War, the Spanish-American War, WWI, WWII, Vietnam, and numerous other politically approved military adventures.

The media not only failed to perform its "watch dog" function over the government related to those military adventures, but by and large it served as a fourth branch of the government by functioning as little more than a shill promoting the position of whoever controlled the White House at a given time.

The same thing is happening today in regards to the multitude of responses by the U.S. government to the events of September 11th based on the unfounded and untrue allegation they were acts of foreign terrorism against this country, when they weren't.

The perpetrators of the events of September 11th committed criminal acts for sure – but the acts themselves were not acts of foreign terrorism, and they don't justify retaliation against "foreigners" or any country based on the false allegation they were. Consequently the entire alleged war on terrorism is a fraudulent illusory sham. That means among other things, that the dropping of over 22,000 bombs on Afghanistan in the fall of 2001 was an abominable crime against humanity by President Bush and other U.S. and British political and military leaders, since it caused the murderous slaughter of 5,000 innocent Afghani's, including women, children and old people. That slaughter of civilians was compounded by the destruction of that country's minimal public health infrastructure that resulted in more needless deaths and suffering of innocent people.

---

[16] "Whoever did plot and plan the 9-11 terrorist attacks, there is no evidence they were working out of Afghanistan. The FBI admits that among thousands of documents discovered in Afghanistan produced by al-Qaeda, "not a single sheet of paper--- not even one computer entry --- mentions any aspect of the Sept. 11 terrorist attacks." [*MSNBC*, May 3, 2002] Even as early as September 23, 2001, the Washington Post reported that al-Qaeda had no connection whatsoever to the 19 hijackers on the aircraft that hit the World Trade Center towers or the Pentagon. According to the story, the CIA and the FBI had been tracking al-Qaeda "cells" inside the U.S. for over two years and characterized their activities as "benign." [*Washington Post*, Sept. 23, 2001] Most of the hijackers were later identified as being Saudi Arabian." Source: http://shadownews.org/archives/911.htm . Fifteen of the nineteen men identified as being involved in the hijackings had Saudi Arabian roots.

[17] Excerpts from Chapter 1 of Mr. Ellsberg's book, in which he talks about the events of August 1964, is at: http://www.ellsberg.net/index.htm .

[18] *Joint Resolution of Congress*, H.J. RES 1145 August 7, 1964. Reporters and journalists that uncritically parrot the official government version of events to their readers, viewers or listeners, are known as *functionaries* in France.

George Seldes wrote extensively on how the news media in the U.S. is beholden to its advertisers and sources of information, and the lengths it will go to in protecting them from adverse publicity. Mr. Seldes' observations are compellingly presented in the documentary about his life: *Tell the Truth and Run: George Seldes and the American Press* (1988), an Academy-Award nominated film by Rick Goldsmith.

[19] "In war, some facts less factual," By Scott Peterson, *The Christian Science Monitor*, September 6, 2002, https://www.csmonitor.com/2002/0906/p01s02-wosc.html

[20] *Id.*

[21] The harm to men and women service people included being afflicted with Gulf War Syndrome, which the federal government may have deliberately made out to be mysterious so as to minimize its financial responsibility to the injuries they suffered.

VI

The USA Patriot Act Only Incidentally Concerns Terrorism

Although Osama bin Laden and al-Qaeda did not engage in terrorism related to the events of September 11th and no evidence has been revealed that they had anything to do with them, and those events have had a virtually negligible effect on how Americans choose to conduct their daily life, there is one area in which those events have been used as a cause célèbre to profoundly affect Americans. They have been used to justify significant modifications to how the federal government relates to people living in the U.S. and other countries in ways that are totally unrelated to the events of September 11th.

While the events of September 11th directly affected the lives of a few tens of thousands of people, the federal government's response to them has impacted the almost three hundred million Americans and hundreds of millions of people in other countries.

The USA Patriot Act of 2001 (UPACT) is one of the two most well-known legislative responses to September 11th that affects how the federal government relates to Americans and "foreigners."[22] Within days after September 11th the U.S. government immediately jumped on the bandwagon of using those events to advocate and push the UPACT through Congress. It was enacted just 6 weeks later on October 24, 2001, without a single congressman or senator having had the opportunity to review the entirety of its contents prior to voting for its enactment. Those legislators were cowed into voting for the UPACT by intimations that only an unpatriotic person would not wholeheartedly support its contents sight unseen.

The reality of the UPACT is that if those elected officials are given the benefit of the doubt that they had good intentions, then they were clearly fooled by President Bush, Attorney General Ashcroft and other officials within the U.S. government into supporting legislation that goes far beyond its trumpeted purpose of being a tool to fight terrorism.[23] The UPACT's preamble clearly states that dealing with terrorism is only one of its *unspecified* many purposes:

AN ACT

To deter and punish terrorist acts in the United States and around the world, *to enhance law enforcement investigatory tools, and for other purposes*.[24] (emphasis added to original)

As the preamble makes plain, the UPACT is shrouded in secrecy because only two of its actual purposes are revealed – and only one of those even facially concerns terrorism. That envelope of secrecy about the unknown number of "other purposes" of the Act that are unspecified may have been the primary reason the text of the Act was concealed from lawmakers until *after* they had voted to enact it.

So contrary to the public exhortations by administration officials that were designed to generate public support for the UPACT before its provisions were publicly disclosed, the Acts preamble plainly reveals that it is only incidentally concerned with deterring and punishing terrorist acts.

Whatever questions there are about the UPACT's mysterious purposes, one thing is known for certain about the broad and extraordinary police powers granted the executive branch in its many provisions related to enhancing "law enforcement investigatory tools, and for other purposes." That is those provisions have no relationship to deterring and punishing terrorism that was the reason used to induce Congressional members to vote for its enactment sight unseen.

It was perhaps unbeknownst to all but a few members of Congress that the UPACT's authors, the U.S. Department of Justice, took advantage of the secrecy surrounding the Act's contents to include the large body of provisions that it openly concedes in the preamble are unrelated to fighting terrorism. The meaning and implications of those provisions has never been publicly disclosed and are still only known by Attorney General John Ashcroft and other administration insiders. In an effort to gain an understanding of the UPACT, a year after its enactment a Senate subcommittee had to resort to threatening to subpoena Attorney General John Ashcroft to answer 50 questions about the meaning of its contents.[25]

The USA Patriot Act's only incidental concern with combating foreign terrorism is consistent with the fact that the events of September 11th were not acts of terrorism by Osama bin Laden associated al-Qaeda Islamic fundamentalists. So it is logical that legislation relying on non-existent foreign terrorist events for its passage would not be particularly concerned with deterring and punishing actual "terrorist acts."

[22] The other is the Homeland Security Act of 2002 signed into law in November 25, 2002. See the entire text of the USA Patriot Act of 2001 on the Electronic Freedom Frontiers website at:
http://www.eff.org/Privacy/Surveillance/Terrorism_militias/20011025_hr3162_usa_patriot_bill.html .

[23] It is impossible for this author to ascribe good intentions to elected officials that vote for *any* legislation they don't understand. Only a fool or a knave would abuse their position of trust and responsibility to do such a thing.

[24] See the text of the USA Patriot Act of 2001 on the Electronic Freedom Frontiers website at:
http://www.eff.org/Privacy/Surveillance/Terrorism_militias/20011025_hr3162_usa_patriot_bill.html .

[25] See e.g., "Sensenbrenner wants answers on act: He threatens to subpoena Ashcroft to get details on antiterror measure," Steve Schultze, *Milwaukee Journal Sentinel*, August 19, 2002.

VII

The Illusion of Homeland Security

More than a year after the events of September 11, 2001, no full scale investigation of what occurred, or who planned and executed those events was begun by any federal agency.[26] Furthermore, although Senate and House committees have broad and far-reaching subpoena powers that enable them to conduct extensive investigations into matters related to the federal government, no committee used those powers to do so prior to passage of the UPACT or for more than a year afterward. In fact, President Bush personally lobbied members of Congress *not* to conduct an investigation into September 11th, claiming it would interfere with, and endanger national security.[27]

Officially then, every proposed course of action and proposed and/or enacted legislation related to the events of September 11th has been based on sheer public speculation about the why and wherefore of what happened. There can consequently be no rational political response to those events, since knowing the answer to who, what, why and how they occurred is critical to formulating a strategy for how to appropriately respond to them.

Yet, while in a state of blindness about the events of September 11th, Congress passed the USA Patriot Act of 2001 just six weeks after they occurred. The UPACT's proponents were able to rush it through Congress because an insufficient number of its members insisted on taking the time to study its provisions. The majority caved into heavy behind the scenes lobbying and public exhortations by its supporters that only unpatriotic Americans could oppose it. Thus, due to the circumstances of its enactment, it can not reasonably be claimed that the UPACT has anything to do with preventing a reoccurrence of events on the scale of September 11th, since its provisions have no known relationship to what underlies those events.

Similarly disassociated from the events of September 11th is the Homeland Security Act of 2002 (HSA) that goes beyond the UPACT by merging such diverse agencies as the INS, the Coast Guard, and Customs into an enormous new cabinet level federal bureaucracy. Given that no detailed investigation has been conducted and hence no supportable conclusions about the why and wherefore of those events has been made, there is no basis to link *any* provision of the HSA or the bureaucracy it creates with an effort to prevent such events from occurring again. Supporting the lack of a link between the HSA and the events of September

11th are two of its key components, one is related to collection of data on Americans, and the other is related to the smallpox inoculation of Americans.

The provision related to the collection of data on Americans authorizes the creation and maintenance of the most extensive database of a country's population ever seriously proposed, much less undertaken.[28] Referred to in the HSA as *Information Analysis and Infrastructure Protection*, the Defense Department's secretive Defense Advanced Research Projects Agency (DARPA) has a budget of $120 million a year to bring such a data collection and analysis program to life.[29] Referred to in the Defense Department as Total Information Awareness (TIA), the program is designed to store and analysis literally every collectable piece of public and private electronic information about a person's life.[30] The information analysis provision of the HSA makes that data of indispensable value to the Homeland Security Department, and for all practical purposes, it would also be available to federal law enforcement agencies. This superized centralized database would accumulate every one of a person's credit card purchases, magazine and newspaper subscriptions, prescriptions, emails sent and received, financial transactions, airplane, train and cruise trips, library books checked out, videos rented, one's driving record, school transcripts, divorce and other court records, even complaints by their neighbors to the police. In addition to centralizing a person's lifetime paper and electronic trail, their biometric information would enable them to be remotely identified, and face recognition technology would make it possible for any surveillance recording they may appear in to be linked to them. This all pervasive "watching" and the personal analysis of a person's life it makes possible, fulfills the sickest fantasies of the most perverted Peeping Tom or Jane.[31]

Yet, there is no identifiable relationship between the centralized collection of this life encompassing data on the nearly 300 million people in the U.S. and the prevention of acts of terrorism. Particularly given that the Total Information Awareness data system would not have contributed to preventing the events of September 11, 2001.[32]

The level of personal intrusiveness authorized in the HSA is only made possible by the government's active funding of advances in computer data storage, retrieval and analysis capabilities.[33] It was too strategically timed to have been coincidental that just *one day prior* to the November 20, 2002 passage of the HSA by the Senate, IBM announced plans to construct a supercomputer for the federal government that is *10 times faster* than any existing computer.[34] Code named Blue Gene/L, the computer will be able to perform 360 trillion mathematical operations a second, and it will be the first of two computers the federal government is paying IBM $290 million to construct.[35] The HSA and its companion Total Information Awareness project exponentially increases the data processing needs of the federal government to incorporate real-time analysis of the many thousands of bits of information compiled on each of the nearly 300 million people in the U.S.

The federal government's intensive level of surveilling Americans epitomized by the HSA far surpasses what George Orwell prophesized in *1984*. In his futuristic society the common folk – known as the Proles – were typically only subject to surveillance by snitches willing to trade information for favors. Similar to the DOJ's nationwide network of several million snitches under its TIPs program.

The other component of the HSA that has no known link to September 11th is Section 304, Subsection C, titled Administration of Counter Measures Against Smallpox. That section has two prongs. The first of those prongs is the compulsory requirement that the smallpox vaccine be administered to any individual or group designated by the Secretary of the Department of Health and Human Services, if he or she "declares an actual *or potential* bio-terrorist *or other kind of incident*."[36] This provision was included, even though the events of September 11th had nothing to do with smallpox, and there has been no credible threat of the U.S. being subjected to a deliberate attempt to spread the smallpox virus. Furthermore, there are compelling scientific and experiential reasons to believe that the smallpox virus poses no potential, much less an actual threat, of causing a disease outbreak in the U.S.[37]

The second prong of the smallpox provision is that anyone harmed by side effects of a mandatory inoculation cannot sue anyone for their injuries: not the government, the person administering the inoculation, or the drug's manufacturer. This provision was inserted even though it is known that at least 3% of everyone receiving the vaccine will suffer serious negative side effects that can include death.[38] A spokesperson for the Association of American Physicians and Surgeons described the smallpox provision of the HSA in the following way:

> "This section will give the Secretary unlimited power to define a real or potential threat, to take any measures he decides and to do it for as long as he wants. It's Alice in Wonderland time again – an emergency is just what he says it is. ... Just what are the 'counter measures' allowed? Forced immunizations? Quarantines? It's not clear, but the powers seem virtually unchecked by any other agency. We need an honest accounting of how this will work. It's too frightening to allow it to be rammed through."[39]

Consistent with the fact that there is no known relationship between any provision of the HSA and the prevention of another event on the scale of September 11th, is that provisions were surreptitiously added to the HSA during the night before the House of Representatives voted to approve it on November 13, 2002, and the text of the HSA was not even made available to the Representatives voting for or against it until *after* they did so.[40] That subterfuge was repeated the following week in the Senate.

On the day of the Senate vote, Senator Robert Byrd (D-WV) expressed his outrage on the floor of the Senate over the way the HSA was being rammed through Congress at blinding speed without any deliberation whatsoever. His incisive comments are worth quoting at length:

> "I remember years ago, when I was in the House of Representatives, sending out a little booklet to the people in my then-congressional district of how our laws are made ...[describes the process of hearings, committees, debate, reports, etc. etc.]... we all remember how those laws are made according to the script as prepared there in those handsome little booklets that we send out. That is how the American people expect this Congress to operate. That is the way we are supposed to operate.
>
> But the way this bill was brought in here, less than 48 hours ago, a brand-new bill. It had not been before any committee. It had undergone no hearings, not this bill. It is a bill on our desks that has 484 pages. There are 484 pages in this bill.
>
> It has not been before any committee. There have been no hearings on this bill. There have been no witnesses who were asked to appear to testify on behalf of the bill or in opposition to it. It did not undergo any such scrutiny.
>
> It was just placed on the Senate Calendar. It was offered as an amendment here. And so here it is before the Senate now. There it is. That is not the way in which our children are taught how we make our laws—not at all.
>
> The American people expect us to provide our best judgment and our best insight into such monumental decisions. This is a far, far cry from being our best. This is not our best. As a matter of fact, it is a mere shadow of our best. Yet we are being asked, as the elected representatives of the American people, those of us who are sent here by our respective States are being asked on tomorrow to invoke closure on these 484 pages.

If I had to go before the bar of judgment tomorrow and were asked by the eternal God what is in this bill, I could not answer God. If I were asked by the people of West Virginia, Senator Byrd, what is in that bill, I could not answer. I could not tell the people of West Virginia what is in this bill.

There are a few things that I know are in it by virtue of the fact that I have had 48 hours, sleeping time included, in which to study this monstrosity, 484 pages. If there ever were a monstrosity, this is it. I hold it in my hand, a monstrosity. I don't know what is in it. I know a few things that are in it, and a few things that I know are in it that I don't think the American people would approve of if they knew what was in there.

Even Senator Lieberman, who is chairman of the committee which has jurisdiction over this subject matter, even he saw new provisions in this legislation as he looked through it yesterday and today. As his staff looked through it, they saw provisions they had not seen before, that they had not discussed before, that had not been before their committee before.

Yet we are being asked on tomorrow to invoke cloture on that which means we are not going to debate in the normal course of things. We are going to have 30 hours of debate. That is it, 30 hours. That is all, 30 hours; 100 Senators, 30 hours of debate.

And this is one of the most far-reaching pieces of legislation I have seen in my 50 years. I will have been in Congress 50 years come January 3... Never have I seen such a monstrous piece of legislation sent to this body. And we are being asked to vote on that 484 pages tomorrow. Our poor staffs were up most of the night studying it. They know some of the things that are in there, but they don't know all of them. It is a sham and it is a shame.

We are all complicit in going along with it. I read in the paper that nobody will have the courage to vote against it. Well, Robert Byrd is going to vote against it because I don't know what I am voting for. That is one thing. And No. 2, it has not had the scrutiny that we tell our young people, that we tell these sweet pages here, boys and girls who come up here, we tell them our laws should have.

This is a hoax. This is a hoax. To tell the American people they are going to be safer when we pass this is to hoax. We ought to tell the people the truth. They are not going to be any safer with that. That is not the truth. I was one of the first in the Senate to say we need a new Department of Homeland Security. I meant that. But I didn't mean this particular hoax that this administration is trying to pander off to the American people, telling them this is homeland security. That is not homeland security. Mr. President, the Attorney General and Director of Homeland Security have told Americans repeatedly there is an imminent risk of another terrorist attack. Just within the past day, or few hours, the FBI has put hospitals in the Washington area, Houston, San Francisco, and Chicago on notice of a possible terrorist threat.

This bill does nothing – not a thing – to make our citizens more secure today or tomorrow. This bill does not even go into effect for up to 12 months. ..."[41]

The Senate ignored Senator Byrd's carefully reasoned concerns based on his 50 years in Congress. On November 20, 2002 the Senate voted 90-9 in favor of the HSA without making a single alteration to the 484 page bill. After making a reasoned analysis of the HSA, Norman D. Livergood, Ph.D, concluded its possible effect on the U.S. is eerily similar to German President Hindenburg's *A Decree of the Reich President for the Protection of the People and State* issued on February 28, 1933.[42] That decree provided the legal foundation necessary to legitimize everything the National Socialist Workers Party, led by Adolf Hitler, did from 1933 to 1945.

The subterfuge surrounding the passage of the HSA is compounded by the fact that its history is a perfect example of the story about the frog in the pot of cold water that is cooked by imperceptible increases in the water temperature to the boiling point. Since at least 1999, the concept of a Homeland Security Department was openly discussed in Washington D.C.'s inner circles of power. One proof of that is homeland security was the underlying theme of the Phase I Report of the U.S. Commission on National Security/21st Century, dated September 15, 1999. Among other things, that report discusses how spectacular terrorist events would counteract diminishing engagement of people with federal politics, the reduced need for a large U.S. military with the end of the Cold War, the growing attitude of people that the U.S. doesn't need to be actively involved in the domestic affairs of other countries, and the trend of Americans to focus on local and state politics.[43] Preparing for a prospective terrorist threat is presented in that report as a crucial antidote to offset trends that would lead to a reduced federal military presence around the world: "In the absence of such a [terrorist] threat, we have experienced mostly periods of heated but inconclusive debate over the American mission in the world."[44]

Evolvement of the Commission's strategy into open advocacy of a Department of Homeland Security was evident in its Phase III Report, issued on February 15, 2001. Titled, *Road Map for National Security: Imperative For Change*, all of the essential structural features of the HSA are outlined in that report issued *seven months* prior to September 11th.[45] One notable exclusion from the HSA is the Commission's mention of using the military for domestic police purposes, which would require repeal of 1878's Posse Comitatus Act.[46] Although the possible repeal of that Act has publicly been mentioned by President Bush and others.

So after years of behind the scenes preparation, President Bush publicly floated the idea of an office of Homeland Security to members of Congress and the American people after September 11th by telling them it was a simple reorganization of existing agencies and it wouldn't cause an increase in federal spending. That seemingly innocuous proposal grew into a 32 page bill creating a new federal Department of Homeland Security. The proposal grew once again into a 282 page bill creating a new federal bureaucracy with a projected annual budget in excess of $3 billion. The bill again grew at the last minute during the night before it was to be voted on by the House of Representatives into a 484-page bill that authorized creation of a massive cabinet level federal bureaucracy controlling two dozen existing federal agencies, and that is estimated to increase federal spending by at least $30 billion.[47] It was in the *dead of that last night* that the provisions were covertly inserted into the HSA authorizing the Information Analysis and Infrastructure Protection and the Administration of Counter Measures Against Smallpox.

Thus the Homeland Security Act mimics the UPACT in two important ways. First, the provisions of neither Act have any known relationship to the events of September 11th nor to the prevention of their reoccurrence. Second, the actual text of both acts was withheld from members of the Congress until the day they were to be voted on – when a no vote, or even a desire to delay voting so its provisions could be studied would have been politically painted by President Bush and his supporters as unpatriotic. By painting anyone as lacking patriotism who even dared to question the wisdom of voting on monumental legislation without knowing its details, the Bush administration borrowed the tactic used by the National Socialists (Nazis) to rally support by the German people for their political policies that included sending military forces into Czechoslovakia, Austria, France, Poland, Greece, etc. This tactic was explained in the following way by Hermann Goering – first inline to succeed Hitler as leader of the Nazi Party – who was tried, convicted and sentenced to death as a war criminal at Nuremberg in 1946:

> "[I]t is the leaders of the country who determine the policy, and it is always a simple matter to drag the people along, whether it is a democracy, or a fascist dictatorship, or a parliament, or a communist dictatorship. Voice or no voice, the people can always be brought to the bidding of the leaders. That is easy. All you have to do is tell them they are being attacked, and denounce the peacemakers for lack of patriotism and exposing the country to danger. It works the same in any country."[48]

It was also convenient for the HSA's proponents that days before the House was to vote on that Bill, an alleged audio recording of Osama bin Laden warning of spectacular attacks against the U.S. exceeding those of September 11th was broadcast on an Arabic television network. The fortuitous timing of that recording's broadcast helped to cement the votes of otherwise wavering Representatives. Although U.S. law enforcement agencies declared at the time it believed the recording was authentic, after the HSA was passed by Congress and days after it was signed into law by President Bush, a group of Swiss voice recognition experts declared it is a near certainty the recording is a fraud. The researchers used sophisticated audio equipment to compare the voice on the recording with twenty known recordings of bin Laden's voice.[49] Yet, whoever created the fraudulent recording had sufficient resources to employ an imposter able to "fool" the Central Intelligence Agency (CIA) – unless that agency was behind the manufacture of the recording.

Consequently, it is a carefully crafted illusion that the HSA has anything to do with preventing terrorism, particularly considering that the events on September 11th underlying the purported need for its passage were not acts of foreign terrorism. Given that the real purpose behind the HSA has been concealed from many members of Congress and the public, it can only be presumed that those reasons are so nefarious that the HSA and the previously enacted UPACT would summarily be rejected if their real purpose was openly acknowledged by their proponents.

[26] On November 27, 2002, almost 15 months after September 11th, 2001, Henry Kissinger was named to be the chairman of a Commission to investigate the events of that day. Of course, given the law enforcement maxim that the trail of a crimes perpetrator(s) grows colder each day that passes, then it is certainly likely that many crucial and important facts related to the events of that day are forever gone. Henry Kissinger abruptly resigned less than three weeks later on December 13, 2002.

[27] *9/11: The Big Lie*, Thierry Meyssan, Carnot Publishing, Paris, FR, 2002, p. 86. On November 27, 2002 Henry Kissinger was named as President Bush's hand-picked choice to head a commission to investigate the events of September 11th. President Bush only agreed to creation of the commission in exchange for the *carte blanc* support of the HSA by key Democratic leaders. President Bush demanded, and was given, the power to appoint the commission's leader. Henry Kissinger's many years in the inner sanctum of government made him the perfect person to oversee an investigation of September 11th that superficially is intended to appear thorough, but which is actually intended to gloss over or ignore the substance of what occurred both visibly and beneath the scenes on that day, and in the days, months, and years leading up to it. Since Henry Kissinger is wanted in several countries, such as Chile, for his crimes against humanity that include the ordering of "hits" on foreign citizens, he owes a significant debt to President Bush. On September 30, 2002 President Bush was able bully the U.N. into approving an exemption of Americans from prosecution in the International Criminal Court (ICC). Without that exemption, the U.S. could possibly be put in the embarrassing position of having to block efforts by the ICC to investigate, and possibly issue an international arrest warrant so it could put Kissinger on trial for the international crimes he allegedly committed. Mr. Kissinger committed those acts while he was the United States Secretary of State under President Nixon, and they were committed in the furtherance of what were perceived as the U.S.'s interests at the time. Kissinger's duplicity between his public persona and his private actions was so complete that he won the Nobel Peace Prize during the time he was ordering "hits" on foreign citizens. Furthermore, as the U.S. Secretary of State, Henry Kissinger played a central role in the Chilean military coup on September 11, 1973 that deposed Constitutionally elected President Salvador Allende, during which at least 3,197 Chileans were killed and over 60,000 were tortured. Kissinger oversaw the funneling of millions of dollars to the military conspirators and the supplying of them with lists of dissidents who after being rounded up, were executed or tortured during their imprisonment. See e.g., "President Names Kissinger To Lead 9/11 Commission," Richard N. Stevenson, *The New York Times*, 11-28-02, pp. A1, 20; "Terrorism in Chile, September 11, 1973," Bill Vann, *The Paper*, Victoria, Australia, Edition 39, October 2002, available at: http://www.thepaper.org.au/issues/039/039terrorism_in_chile_september_11_197 3.html; *The Trial of Henry Kissinger*, Christopher Hitchens, Verso, 2001; and, "Americans Spared War Crimes Court," (Brussels, Belgium) *The Guardian Unlimited*, October 1, 2002.

The agreement permits U.S. citizens, such as Henry Kissinger, to avoid prosecution for genocide, crimes against humanity and war crimes in the ICC that citizens of other countries, such as Slobodan Milosevic, are unable to avoid. The article states in part: "Defusing a trans-Atlantic spat, the European Union agreed

Monday to spare U.S. citizens the fate of standing trial on war crimes charges in the newly created International Criminal Court."

The U.S. government has struggled to justify its massive annual military expenditures since the Soviet Union, AKA The Evil Empire, evaporated as the boogeyman Americans supposedly needed to be protected from. It can be surmised that Henry Kissinger's job as the head of the 9/11 Commission is to produce a report about September 11th that sustains the illusion that the U.S. is vulnerable and likely to be the target of foreign terrorism, since that threat is required to justify waging a perpetual war against non-existent "terrorism" that is necessary for the U.S. military to maintain, and even increase its expenditures in a time of relative peace in the world. The perpetual war against non-existent terrorism, or which may artificially be generated as a response to the U.S.'s aggression, is reminiscent of the perpetual war in Orwell's 1984 that served the same purpose.

On December 13, 2002 Henry Kissinger abruptly quit as Chairman of the 9/11 Commission on the grounds that he couldn't compromise clients of his consulting company by publicly disclosing who they are, which is a requirement of service on the 9/11 Commission. See e.g., "Kissinger Pulls Out as Chief Of Inquiry Into 9/11 Attacks," David Firestone, *The New York Times*, December 14, 2002, Sec. A, p. 1, col. 1.

[28] The data section of the Homeland Security Act is: *Title II – Information Analysis and Infrastructure Protection.* For an explanation of everything entailed by Title II, see e.g., "You Are A Suspect," William Safire, *The New York Times*, Nov. 14, 2002; and, "A Supersnoop's Dream," Audrey Hudson, *The Washington [D.C.] Times*, Nov. 15, 2002. The HSA can also be used to turn state drivers licenses into de facto national I.D. cards by linking them to Title II's database collection and analysis system.

[29] The Information Analysis provision of the Homeland Security Act and the Total Information Awareness program are inexorably linked in reality, whatever disconnection there may appear to be on the surface. When the Homeland Security Act was passed, the Total Information Awareness project was funded with $120 million to carry out its surveillance of Americans. For an explanation of DARPA's role in driving the development of computer technology that is enabling the systematic obliteration of liberty in America, see this author's essay: *Rule By Punch Cards or: How Computers Are a Menace to Liberty*, Hans Sherrer (October 2002), available at: www.forejustice.org/ms/rule_by_punch_cards.htm.

[30] Under Homeland Security Act Section 201(d)(1), it is the responsibility of those entrusted with executing the Information Analysis and Infrastructure Protection provision: "To access, receive, and analyze law enforcement information, intelligence information, and other information from agencies of the Federal Government, State and local government agencies (including law enforcement agencies), and private sector entities, and to integrate such information."

[31] TIA is envisioned to accomplish this by utilizing software from Syntek Technologies, that markets a commercial version of the software known as Genoa. Syntek Technologies was the previous employer of John Poindexter, the director of the TIA project. See e.g., "The U.S. Spymaster: John Poindexter's Information

Awareness Office wants to read your email," Eric Johnson, *Coast Weekly*, Monterey, CA, Dec. 5, 2002, at:

http://www.*coastweekly*.com/article.asp?section=results&ref=8489.

[32] There is a significant body of evidence that intelligence gathering tools available to the FBI prior to September 11, 2001 enabled the agency to identify people that could be planning to commit violent criminal acts in the U.S. and other countries. Coleen Rowley, an FBI whistleblower disclosed that prior to September 11th her FBI superiors and DOJ officials interfered with her investigation of people possibly planning violent criminal activity in the U.S. See e.g., "Coleen Rowley's Memo to FBI Director Robert Mueller: An edited version of the agent's 13-page letter," *Time Magazine*, May 21, 2002, at:

http://www.time.com/time/nation/article/0,8599,249997,00.html .

Time Magazine named Coleen Rowley and the women that blew the whistle on Enron and WorldCom as their People of The Year for 2002. The fact that Coleen Rowley and other FBI agents (two of those agents were interviewed on ABC's *Primetime Live* on December 19, 2002) were instructed by superiors in Washington DC to stand down in following suspicious leads prior to September 11th substantiates that elements within the federal government may have been intimately involved in the planning and execution of those events, since there is no conceivable reason for those agents to have been diverted from carrying out investigations, unless they would have led to the discovery of those internal elements prior to the execution of those events.

[33] See e.g., an analysis by this author of the direct relationship between the federal government and the development of the computer as an instrument information collection and surveillance in *Rule By Punch Cards or: How Computers Are a Menace to Liberty*, to be published in 2003 in an anthology about the danger national ID cards pose to the liberty of Americans, available at:

www.forejustice.org/ms/rule_by_punch_cards.htm .

[34] "I.B.M. Plans a Computer That Will Set Power Record," John Markoff, *The New York Times*, Technology Section, November 19, 2002. The publicly announced purpose of the computer is to do simulations related to nuclear war and nuclear waste.

[35] *Id.*

[36] *Smallpox Provisions Hidden In Homeland Security Bill*, Association of American Physicians and Surgeons, November 14, 2002, FreeRepublic.com at: http://www.freerepublic.com/focus/news/789101.posts (emphasis added).

[37] See e.g., "Term Limits: the meaninglessness of "WMD," Gregg Easterbrook, *The New Republic*, October 7, 2002, pp. 22-25, esp. 24-25. Mr. Easterbrook relates that when the Smallpox virus from a Soviet bioweapons lab in Aralsk, Kazakhstan got loose in 1971, only 3 people died in an area of Russia that had such poor public health that the life expectancy of men was only 40 years. The public health in the U.S. is significantly higher, and it is possible that if a comparable release occurred in this country no one would have died. However, it is known that at least 3% of everyone given the Smallpox vaccine suffers serious negative side-effects, including death.

[38] *Id.*

[39] *Smallpox Provisions Hidden In Homeland Security Bill* quoting AAPS spokeswoman Kathryn Serkes.

[40] *Oppose the New Homeland Security Bureaucracy!*, Rep. Ron Paul (TX), November 13, 2002, http://lewrockwell.com/paul/paul61.html

[41] Senator Byrd's comments are available from numerous locations, including: http://www.rense.com/general31/abila.htm .

[42] Professor Livergood's website is at: http://www.hermes-press.com/nazification_step3.htm. The decree invoked Article 48 of the Weimer Constitution, which allowed for suspension in time of an emergency of the multitude of rights that constitutionally protected Germans from the arbitrarily exercise of power by the federal government.

[43] See e.g., *New World Coming: American Security In The 21st Century: Supporting Research and Analysis*, The U.S. Commission on National Security/21st Century, Phase I: , September15, 1999, p. 125. Available at: http://www.nssg.gov/NWR_A.pdf .

[44] *Id.*

[45] This report can be read at the Commission's official website: http://www.nssg.gov/PhaseIIIFR.pdf

[46] 18 U.S.C. 1385. See, Phase I Report of the U.S. Commission on National Security/21st Century, dated September 15, 1999, p. 129.

[47] See the National Taxpayer's Union website at: http://www.ntu.org/features/sotu/SOTU2002graph.php3. Among the several dozen federal agencies coming under the control of the Department of Homeland Security are the Coast Guard, Customs, and the INS. The budgetary increase these agencies will receive is indicated by the fact that none of them objected to being brought under the Homeland Security umbrella.

[48] Nazi leader Hermann Goering, interviewed by Gustave Gilbert during the Easter recess of the Nuremberg trials, 18 April 1946, quoted in Gilbert's book *Nuremberg Diary.*

[49] "Bin Laden tape 'created by imposter,'" (Staff and agencies), *Guardian Unlimited,* London, November 29, 2002.

VIII

A Historical Perspective of How September 11th Has Been Used To Undermine The Liberty Of Americans

Consistent with the fact that the events of September 11, 2001 were not acts of foreign terrorism is the fact that there is nothing inherent about those events that by any stretch of the imagination threatens the national security of the U.S., the personal security or freedom of Americans, or the American way of life. However, all of those things are accomplished by the artificial fear of terrorism generated by the response of federal officials and politicians to the events of September 11. The federal government's saber rattling against Iraq in the absence of any provocation, has endangered Americans by making the U.S. subject to possible retaliation.[50] Furthermore, the security, freedom and way of life of all but the wealthiest Americans is endangered by the USA Patriot Act that arguably does nothing to prevent terrorism, but unquestionably includes provisions that grant the federal government the power to pry into every aspect of a person's life and deprive them of the basic protections afforded a criminal suspect by simply labeling the person as a suspected terrorist.

The events of September 11 have been used by politically influential forces to serve as a crucial stepping stone for the federal government to openly alter its public relationship with Americans. The USA Patriot Act's provisions that effectively suspend application of the Bill of Rights to an American classified by the federal government as a suspected terrorist or enemy combatant, or a sympathizer of either, are a visible representation of the federal government's brazen assumption of the role as a trampler of those rights, and not their protector. When the power of the government is unchecked by a recognition that a person has fundamental rights inseparable from their existence as a human being, its exercise of power against that person is unlimited. The UPACT does that.

Although unintended by its authors, the UPACT has served as a much-needed reminder that the Bill of Rights is philosophically inconsistent with the Constitution it is appended to.

The Constitution creates a federal government whose power is not limited by any external authority.[51] In contrast, the Bill of Rights symbolically shields American's from the wanton exercise of governmental power inconsistent with its enabling provisions. Consequently, the Bill of Rights' restraints and mandates related to the use of governmental power against individual Americans is irreconcilable with the Constitution grant of unlimited power against those very same people.[52] That fundamental conflict is precisely why a Bill of Rights was deliberately excluded from being embodied in the Constitution. Furthermore, its authors and other supporters adamantly opposed including an enumeration of the rights of Americans, since that could interfere with the exercise of the government's power against them. The Founding Fathers wanted no part of a Bill of Rights precisely because its inclusion would have checked employment of the federal government's power against Americans in a way that was carefully avoided from being possible by any other Constitutional provision.[53]

It is a matter of historical record that the Constitution's authors and supporters were vehemently opposed to incorporating a declaration of rights in that document. They were so opposed that they *unanimously refused* to do so when it was drafted and submitted to the thirteen independent nation-states for approval. Those proceedings are recounted in *Creating the Bill of Rights: The Documentary Record from the First Federal Congress*:

> "At the 1787 Federal Convention in Philadelphia George Mason of Virginia and Edbridge Gerry of Massachusetts had proposed that the Constitution include a bill of rights to reassure the people that the vastly strengthened federal government would not oppress them and to secure individual rights for the longterm. *The convention refused unanimously* – a critical error that almost proved fatal to ratification. Antifederalist Richard Henry Lee of Virginia unsuccessfully attempted to attach several amendments to the Constitution in September, before the Confederation Congress submitted it to the states for ratification."[54]

The ten amendments that comprise the Bill of Rights were appended to the Constitution *years* after it was written, approved by the Convention's delegates and submitted to the states for ratification. Public support for the Constitution sans a Bill of Rights was so weak that a significant majority of Americans – estimated to be upwards of 75% – were opposed to its adoptions as a replacement for the Articles of Confederation.[55] As the Constitution's opponents – known as the Antifederalists – passionately pointed out, the Constitution places the people in a position of overt servitude to whoever controls the federal government. Absent the restrictions of a Bill of Rights, the Constitution permits the exercise of unchecked power by whoever is in control against their political opponents and unpopular minorities.[56]

In plain language the Constitution is neither a document promoting human liberty, nor was it intended as such. On the contrary, it was designed so Americans would be subject to absolute control by the government of the United States and whoever handles the reins of its power at any given moment.

As would be expected under those circumstances, the Constitution's champions were the political heavyweights and wealthy people of the day: the very people who stood to benefit the most from its enactment and whose connections would generally shield them from needing to worry about the lack of a Bill of Rights. The Antifederalists on the other hand, understood the corrupting influence of power on the most well intentioned person. William Pitt the Elder expressed this concept in a speech to the House of Lords on January 9, 1770: "Unlimited power is apt to corrupt the minds of those who possess it."[57]

Powers corrupting influence means power can never be trusted with those who seek it. Power seekers, which included the Constitution's proponents, are the people most in need of having their conduct held in check by the symbolic shield provided by a declaration of rights. Unlike the Founding Fathers, the Antifederalists grasped the full import of the maxim that no more power should be granted to one's friends than to one's worst enemy – and they clearly saw the supporters of the Constitution for what the were: the enemies of liberty. The Founding Fathers had a general distaste for those outside their power clique.

Given the Constitution's absence of a Bill of Rights, it isn't surprising that many of the most vociferous advocates for liberation of the American colonies from England, including Patrick Henry and George Mason, were also the most passionate Antifederalist opponents of the Constitution. The Antifederalists were well aware a Bill of Rights is spiritually aligned with the concepts of human autonomy, personal worth, individual dignity, and a decentralized and accountable government.[58] In stark contrast, the Constitution is spiritually aligned with the idea of an all-powerful centralized state to which all but the most financially able and politically connected must blindly kowtow.

The most renowned public speaker of his day, Patrick Henry is most well known to American's today for his resounding proclamation in 1775 of "Give Me Liberty or Give me Death!" Thirteen years later, after the American colonies had firmly been established as separate nations loosely aligned with each other by the Articles of Confederation, Patrick Henry summoned all of his considerable oratory skill and powers of persuasion to convey the danger posed to the liberty of the American people by the Constitution, the country of the United States it created, the subjugation of the independent American nation/states to it, and the federal government it authorized to administer its affairs.[59]

In a speech on June 5, 1788 Patrick Henry described the drive to institute the Constitution as "a revolution as radical as that which separated us from Great Britain."[60] He continued on to eloquently warn:

> "Revolutions like this have happened in almost every country in Europe: Similar examples are to be found in ancient Greece and ancient Rome: Instances of the people losing their liberty by their own carelessness and the ambition of a few."[61]

Among the dangerous aspects of the silent revolution embodied in the Constitution was the thirteen independent American nation-states would effectively surrender their national sovereignty by merging into a super nation-state, and the liberty of Americans would become subservient to the federal government it created.[62] The Antifederalist's concerns were in acknowledgement of the obvious: the United States created by the Constitution would smother the autonomy of the people and the States it was overlaid on top of, and with it the liberty of Americans.

It isn't well known today that America is not the same thing as the United States, and America predates the United States. Patrick Henry clarified this when on June 7, 1788 he stated in a speech prior to creation of the United States: "The voice of tradition, I trust, will inform posterity of our struggles for freedom. If our descendents be worthy of the name of Americans, they will preserve and hand down to their latest posterity, the transactions of the present times; ... The first thing I have at heart is American liberty; the second thing is American Union, and I hope the people of Virginia endeavor to preserve that Union."[63] The Union he was referring to was the loose coalition of the 13 independent nation states authorized by the Articles of Confederation then in effect.

The Constitution's scheme of creating a central government that in principle could exercise virtually unlimited power against those within its domain was abhorrent to a lover of liberty like Patrick Henry, who warned all who would listen: "Guard with jealous attention the public liberty. Suspect every one who approaches that jewel."[64] The people he was referring to as needing to be suspected for their sabotage of liberty, were the men today referred to as the Founding Fathers. The Constitution's haughty answer to the ageless question posed by Juvenal – "Who guards the guardians?" – was no one.[65]

Patrick Henry continued his verbal barrage on June 7, 1788 when he warned of the unseen but real danger the proposed Constitution posed to the liberty of common Americans:

> "And yet who knows the dangers that this new system may produce; they are out of the sight of the common people: They cannot foresee latent consequences: I dread the operation of it on the middling and lower class of people: It is for them I fear the adoption of this system."[66]

George Mason, author of the 1776 Virginia Bill of Rights that the eventual federal Bill of Rights was modeled after, was an Antifederalist as fervent in his written opposition to the Constitution as Patrick Henry was in his verbal opposition.[67]

It was in response to the Anti-federalists pointed exposure of the Constitution's provisions impairing the liberty of Americans and the autonomy of the independent nation-states, that the Federalist Papers were written to try and assuage the widespread fear of the powerful centralized government *that would* be created by the Constitution. Consistent with the maxim that what is pawned off as history isn't the truth of what happened so much as it is what the winners want people to think happened, the Federalist Papers remain well known while the voluminous reasoned arguments of the Constitution's Antifederalist opponents are relegated to being preserved in a few books and known to relatively few people.

Alexander Hamilton was a primary behind the scenes architect of the Constitution. Hamilton was also the principle author of The Federalist Papers used to drum up support for it when it was headed for rejection by the state legislatures. As the Constitution's spiritual Godfather, Hamilton's quest to create an all-powerful central federal government is amply indicated by his unrequited desire for the United States to be ruled by a *King* – not a President – and the First Bank of the United States he founded in 1791 while serving as the first Secretary of the Treasury, was a quasi-private/public commercial bank that was the conceptual forerunner of the Federal Reserve created in 1913.[68]

So even though it is not widely known today, there was fierce opposition to the Constitution throughout the thirteen colonies by those who loved liberty. Their most basic fear was it served as a blueprint for the creation of an authoritarian federal government that would suppress the liberty of the common person in America.[69] After realizing the depth of public opposition to the Constitution could block its ratification, its proponents finally caved in and agreed to the political compromise of appending a Bill of Rights to it. They won the war to ratify the Constitution by conceding their battle to exclude a Bill of Rights. More than *four years* after the Constitutional Convention the Bill of Rights was ratified on December 15, 1791. For more than 200 years those original ten amendments have been the gadfly like nuisance to the wielders of federal power that the Founding Fathers desperately wanted to avoid.

The UPACT undermines what Patrick Henry and other advocates of liberty insisted on in exchange for their reluctant support for adoption of the Constitution: it provides for suspension of the protections afforded by the Bill of Rights and its check on the exercise of unlimited governmental power against Americans. The UPACT's Section 802 – Definition of Domestic Terrorism – also makes those provisions easier to apply to ordinary Americans. It does that by radically altering the statutory definition in 18 United States Code §2331(a) of what can be considered as domestic terrorism to potentially cover non-violent activities of virtually all concerned Americans that voice disapproval of local, state or federal government policies. This could potentially include the writer of a letter to the editor of a newspaper or magazine, a caller to a radio program or the office of an elected official, a media commentator, or a peaceful marcher. It would not be an act of prognostication to predict that the UPACT will be used against such people at some point, because it makes no distinction between peaceful political and social critics, and alleged violent terrorists.

Patrick Henry, George Mason and other Anti-federalists are rolling over in their graves and their ghosts are howling, because the UPACT is representative of legislation that brings their worst fears about the federal government into reality.

The wake of September 11th has left the liberties of Americans assaulted from multiple angles, not the least of which is the UPACT that literally reads like a document that could have been written by German lawyers during the Nazi era.[70] On the state level there have also been laws of varying kinds enacted since September 11th narrowing protections against invasion of one's privacy by government agents. Liberty is dependent on respect for privacy, so any impairment by the government of one's privacy is an attack by it on one's liberty.[71]

As disturbing as they may be, the recent actions by the federal government are not without precedent. The acronym Nazi was shorthand for the National Socialist German Workers' Party (NSDAP). The Nazi's were neither a rogue organization nor did they lack popular support. Quite to the contrary, they were a political party duly elected to power like the Republicans and Democrats are in this country. Furthermore, the legal system and civil service apparatus maintained their pre-Nazi functions throughout the years the Nazi Party controlled the German government, and continued to do so after it was removed from power. The Nazis depended on the seemingly normal people in the German bureaucracy to efficiently carry out their political policies. One example of this is that 10 years after WWII ended, about 50% of Germany's judges had served as judges during the Nazi era, and had dutifully enforced the laws that enabled all the horrors of that era to be "legally" committed.

It is also worth remembering that not only was the German Constitution of Hitler's era modeled after the U.S. Constitution, but so was Soviet Russia's.[72] The Nazi's weren't slowed in the slightest by the German Constitution from victimizing many millions of people, even though it offered *more* written protections than does the U.S. Constitution.[73] Likewise, the Soviet's weren't deterred in the slightest by their Constitution from murdering over 43 million innocent people during the almost 30 year reign of terror under Stalin, even though the Soviet Constitution provided many more protections for individuals than either the German or U.S. Constitution.[74]

The foregoing makes it clear that there is *nothing* in the U.S. Constitution proper to prevent a Nazi or Stalinist like police state and reign of terror in this country. Although the Bill of Rights appended to it poses no physical bar, it does serve as a symbolic shield that at least give pause to those wanting to do so. That was the premise in *The R Document* by best-selling novelist Irving Wallace. His book's scenario is that suspension of the Bill of Rights, the internment of dissident Americans in concentration camps, and a declaration of martial law would be the federal government's response to a national security crisis manufactured out of thin air by a federal law enforcement agency with the initials: F.B.I. Mr. Wallace's book was published in 1976.

It is eerily reminiscent of *The R Document's* theme that the UPACT provides conditions under which the Bill of Rights application to a U.S. citizen can be suspended, and they can thus be treated similar to dissidents in Nazi Germany, Soviet Russian and Communist China. This aspect of the UPACT has not gone unnoticed by astute observers. On August 14, 2002 the *Los Angeles Times* reported on Attorney General John Ashcroft's "hellish vision" of setting up concentration camps for Americans stripped of their protections under the Bill of Rights by being administratively labeled as an "enemy combatant;" and numerous government agencies, including FEMA, are known to have plans ready for activation when martial law is declared.[75] After realizing the implications of the federal government's actions justified by the events of September 11th, one can't be faulted for having the response of exclaiming: "Yikes!"

Remarkably, the foreign press openly recognizes what is largely concealed by the media in this country: the philosophical shift that has publicly occurred between government in the U.S. and Americans since September 11th.

It is also noteworthy that by doing nothing to impact the Constitution proper, the UPACT reveals that all that is necessary for the U.S. to function as a *de facto* police state is for the federal government to be freed one way or another from the symbolic restraint of the Bill of Rights.

The UPACT's authors were devilishly ingenious by leaving the Bill of Rights intact, but nullifying it through suspension of its application to a person simply labeled by the government as a suspected terrorist or supporter of terrorism. It is childishly naïve to think that such perfection in the UPACT's design is accidental. That is as likely as the duplication of the Mona Lisa by a blindfolded monkey wielding a paintbrush.

The philosophical consistency between the UPACT and the Constitution sans a Bill of Rights is no mere coincidence. Known as Federalists, the Constitution's founding fathers hated the very concept of a Bill of Rights and successfully excluded it from the body of the Constitution. Similarly, key public supporters of the UPACT, including Attorney General John Ashcroft, arc members of the Federalist Society headquartered in Washington DC that is dedicated to promoting the ideals expressed in the Constitution. Thus the Federalists of today are continuing the revolution against human liberty that the Anti-federalists warned is embodied in the Constitution.

The UPACT is a huge step to severing the restraints imposed on the federal government by the declaration of rights that Patrick Henry, George Mason and other advocates of liberty valiantly fought to have it bound by. Although at this point it is academic, the UPACT is another validation of the Anti-federalists worst fears about how liberty in America could easily be victimized by normal operations of the centralized federal government created by the Constitution. That lesson was hastened by those who have made every effort to politically and financially profit from falsely characterizing the events of September 11 as foreign terrorism.[76]

[50] Based on his six years as a U.N. weapons inspector, Scott Ritter has pointed out that the secrecy of the Iraqi government about some its activities has nothing to do with concealing weapons development programs, manufacturing facilities, or stockpiled weapons. Rather, it is concealing Saddam Hussein's security process that keeps him safe from assassination by the CIA or other clandestine groups funded by the U.S. government. A 90 minute talk he gave on October 5, 2002 about these and other subjects related to Iraq can be listened to at: www.forejustice.org/audio/scott_ritter_10-05-02.mp3.

[51] See e.g., an analysis of the U.S. Constitution from this perspective in *The Constitution of No Authority* by Lysander Spooner in *The Lysander Spooner Reader*, Lysander Spooner with an Introduction by George H. Smith, Fox & Wilkes, 1992.

[52] The vehemence of the Founding Fathers opposition to a Bill of Rights might have been tempered if they had not overlooked that it serves one crucial function consistent with their aim to create a government of absolute power: it supports the illusion that the government's power is not *de facto* unlimited, when in its absence that illusion completely evaporates like a morning mist at the break of dawn.

[53] The one provision that some people may try and claim contradicts this is Article 1, Section 9 of the Constitution. That provision forbids the suspension of *habeas corpus* except, "when in Cases of Rebellion or Invasion the public safety may require it." To make such a claim would be deceptive, however, because *habeas corpus* is a protection against *illegal* imprisonment, by providing for judicial review of a person's jailing when they contend there is no legal authority for it. Consequently the Constitution's habeas corpus provision provides no protection against an imprisonment considered legal. This was confirmed less than 10 years after the adoption of the Constitution by the passage of the Alien and Sedition Act that resulted in the "legal" imprisonment of numerous political enemies of the Federalists that were in power. The *habeas corpus* provision provided no relief to them, just as it provides no support for a person jailed under a provision of the UPACT. On November 18, 2002, the constitutionality of the UPACT was upheld by the unanimous vote of a secretive appeals court panel of three federal appeals court judges that were hand-picked by U.S. Supreme Court Chief Justice William Rehnquist. The three judges reversed a unanimous 7-0 vote by all the federal judges on the secret Foreign Intelligence Surveillance Court that the UPACT's wiretapping and information sharing provisions among federal agencies were unconstitutional. See e.g., "Judges uphold wider use of wiretaps: Expanded foreign surveillance allowed," Lyle Denniston (*The Boston Globe*), *Seattle Post-Intelligencer*, Nov. 19, 2002, Nation Section. See also, "Secret Court OKs Broad Wiretap Powers," Deborah Charles, Reuters/Washington, November 18, 2002, available on the Findlaw.com website. Justice Rehnquist, who hand-picked the three appeals court judges, was also one of the five Supreme Court judges that ruled in Bush's favor in *Bush v. Gore* (2000) the decision that effectively amounted to the Supreme Court's appointment of George Bush as President. See e.g., *The Betrayal of America: How the Supreme Court Undermined the Constitution and Chose the President* by Vincent Bugliosi, forward by Gerry Spence, Thunder's Mouth Press / Nation Books ; ISBN: 156025355X, May 2001.

[54] *Creating the Bill of Rights: The Documentary Record from the First Federal Congress*, edited by Helen E. Veit, Kenneth R. Bowling and Charlene Bangs Bickford, John Hopkins University Press, Baltimore and London, 1991, ix. (emphasis added to original). It is pertinent to mention in the context of discussing the opposition of the Founding Fathers to a declaration of rights that there is some spiritual discontinuity between the Constitution and the Declaration of Independence. That is indicated by the fact the former document was only signed by 3 of the 56 signers of the latter document. Contrary to a popular misconception, Thomas Jefferson had no role in drafting the Constitution, he was in France during that period of time, but he did write to James Madison that the Convention had no right to draft a Constitution that would profess to have a life of more than 20 years, since one generation had no right to even make a pretense of legally binding the one that would follow it. The three signers of both documents were Roger Sherman of Connecticut, and Robert Morris and Benjamin Franklin of Pennsylvania.

[55] In stark contrast with the Constitution, the Articles of Confederation respected the national sovereignty of the thirteen colonial nation-states that it loosely tied together by assuring relatively free trade and non-aggression between them.

[56] For the take of the Constitution's opponents about this, see e.g., *The Antifederalists*, ed. by Cecelia M. Kenyon, Northeastern University Press, Boston, 1985 reprint of 1966 edition with a new forward by Gordon S. Wood). At p. xciii she wrote:

> "That a Bill of Rights was needed not only to protect the people from their government but also to protect individuals and minorities from the will of the majority was stated explicitly by James Winthrop. In refuting the federalist argument that Bill of Rights were not necessary in republican governments, he replied: "that the sober and industrious part of the community should be defended from the rapacity and violence of the vicious and idle. A bill of rights, therefore, ought to set forth the purposes for which the compact is made, and serves to secure the minority against the usurpation and tyranny of the majority. ... The experience of mankind has proved the prevalence of a disposition to use power wantonly. It is therefore as necessary to defend an individual against the majority in a republic as against the "King in a monarchy."" [fn. 133: #133 Agrippa Letters, Ford Essays, p. 117. See also Elliot, III, 499, for a similar statement from William Grayson], at p. xciii.

[57] Lord Acton made his similar, but better known phrasing of the same concept 117 years later in a letter to Bishop Mandell Creighton dated April 3, 1887: "Power tends to corrupt, and absolute power corrupts absolutely. Great men are almost always bad man."

[58] It is worth noting that the most passionate of the Antifederalists were not among those that signed the Declaration of Independence. This is explained by a little known spiritual affinity between that document and the Constitution. In 1772 England's Lord Chief Justice Mansfield ruled that English law does not support slavery and ordered that all slavery in England was illegal. Since the colonies legal system was directly based on English law, the freeing of the hundreds of thousands

of slaves in the American colonies was a foregone event waiting to happen. The only way to prevent the freeing of the slaves was for the American colonies to break their direct political dependency on England. The movers and shakers behind the Independence of the American colonies from England exhibited mind-numbing hypocrisy by publicly proclaiming love for liberty while behind the scenes they worked to preserve the institution of slavery. The benefits of cheap slave labor infected the entire colonial economic structure. For example, while far removed geographically from the slave plantations of the South, the New England textile trade depended on their cheap cotton to produce economical finished products. The hypocrisy of the men behind the Declaration of Independence's bold proclamations of human liberty is shown by the personal history of its primary author, Thomas Jefferson. He was a life-long slave owner who didn't liberate the slaves that maintained his Monticello estate because he couldn't afford to maintain it without their "free" labor that only cost him the expense of their minimal upkeep. In other words, he failed to put his bold words of freedom into action in his own life because it would have reduced the style of living to which he had become accustomed.

It is historical fact that if the colonies had not revolted against England, the slaves in America would have been legally emancipated many decades before they were. It is also worth pondering that if the South had not entered into a war with the North that the institution of slavery would have continued on for an unknown number of decades, since the Supreme Court, Congress and Abraham Lincoln were all content to allow the institution to continue as it had for hundreds of years so long as the South was agreeable to paying exorbitant import tariffs on manufactured goods. In other words, the abolition of slavery in the U.S. had nothing to do with elevated moral principles, but pragmatic economic considerations.

The history of slavery in the U.S. and the support of it by a many decades long succession of economic and political leaders is important in the context of what is happening in the U.S. today. The same men that viciously fought to prevent the Constitution's constriction by a declaration of rights incorporated slavery as a salient feature of that document. That same mindset is evident today by the proponents of the Patriot Act and the Homeland Security Act that can only be executed as they are intended if the American people are de facto presumed to have no rights or protections as human beings that are beyond the reach of the government. That is, the UPACT and the HSA depend on Americans to literally be viewed as, and treated like rightless slaves.

[59] See e.g., *The Anti-Federalist Papers and the Constitutional Convention Debates*, edited by Ralph Ketcham, Mentor, Penguin Group, New York, 1986, pp. 201, 208. Patrick Henry said in the speech: "Guard with jealous attention the public liberty. Suspect every one who approaches that jewel. ... Revolutions like this have happened in almost every country in Europe: Similar examples are to be found in ancient Greece and ancient Rome: Instances of the people losing their liberty by their own carelessness and the ambition of a few. ... Yet, there is another thing it will as effectually do: it will oppress and ruin the people." (201) ... "And yet who knows the dangers that this new system may produce; they are out of the sight of the common people: They cannot foresee latent consequences: I dread the operation of it on the middling and lower class of people: It is for them I fear the adoption of this system. ... I see great jeopardy in this new Government. I see none from our present

    A Historical Perspective of How September 11th Has Been Used To Undermine The Liberty of Americans

one:" (208).

Under the Article of Confederation, the independent nation/states of Colonial America had much more autonomy than do European countries that are signatories to the European Union of today. One example of their autonomy was that the Colonial nations of Massachusetts, New York, Virginia, et al did not have a mandated common currency.

[60] In a speech before the Virginia Ratifying Convention. *Id.* at 199.

[61] *Id.* at 201.

[62] The submergence of sovereignty by the American states under the Constitution into a super nation-state called The United States was similar to what occurred during the 1800s when small independent nation/states were absorbed into what because the super nation-state known as Germany.

[63] *Id.* at 212.

[64] *The Anti-Federalist Papers and the Constitutional Convention Debates,* at 201.

[65] Addressing the decadence, erosion of individual rights, and decline of public morality in the Roman Empire about 120 A.D., the satirist Juvenal asked pointedly in his Sixth Satire "quis custodiet ipsos custodies", or, "Who guards the guardians?"

[66] *Id.* at 208. Patrick's Henry's fears of the latent powers imbedded in the Constitution that could be used to destroy any pretense of liberty in the U.S., are perfectly realized in both the HSA and the UPACT that are discussed in later chapters. The overt subjugated state of Americans to the federal government is the given principle underlying those legislative enactments that are abhorrent to the memory of those who fought in the American Revolution and all lovers of liberty since, up to the present day.

[67] See e.g., *George Mason,* Encyclopedia Britannica, at: http://search.eb.com/eb/article?eu=79743&tocid=0&query=mason%2C%20george. Mason's Virginia Declaration of Rights is credited with "being the first authoritative formulation of the doctrine of inalienable rights."

[68] See e.g., Alexander Hamilton, *Encyclopedia Britannica* at: http://search.eb.com/eb/article?eu=39835&tocid=0&query=hamilton%2C%20alexander

[69] *The Anti-Federalist Papers and the Constitutional Convention Debates*, edited by Ralph Ketcham, Mentor, published by the Penguin Group, New York, 1986; and, *The Anti-Federalists*, Herbert Storing, University of Chicago Press, 1985. Note: These books present, in the words of the men who lived at the time of the Constitutional Convention of 1787, the fierce opposition that existed in the thirteen colonies to adoption of the United States Constitution and the centralized federal government it created. Their worst fears about the federal government's inherent rapaciousness was evident for all to see only a few years later. In 1794 George Washington led an army of 13,000 against Americans in Western Pennsylvania who refused to pay the federal excise tax on whiskey they produced and sold. Known as the Whiskey Rebellion – Washington's swift crushing of the dissidents cemented the power of the newly installed federal government. See e.g., *The Whiskey Rebellion,* Thomas P. Slaughter, Oxford University Press, 1986. There is a website devoted to The Whiskey Rebellion at: www.whiskeyrebellion.org

[70] The legal profession enthusiastically assisted the Nazi's with implementation of their political policies. On German Day in November 1933, for example, Adolf Hitler was told by Hans Franc at a rally of 20,000 lawyers in Leipzig, "you can rely on your German lawyers!" Source: http://hoffmannverlag.schiff.bei.t-online.de/irrtum_2.html .

[71] "[T]*he right to be let alone – the most comprehensive of rights and the right most valued by civilized men.*" is how Justice Brandeis summarized the intertwining relationship between privacy and liberty in his dissent in *Olmstead v. U.S.*, 277 U.S. 438, 479 (1928). That was the first case in which the Supreme Court gave its stamp of approval to the wire tapping of private telephone conversations by government agents. Justice Brandeis wrote: "The makers of our Constitution undertook to secure conditions favorable to the pursuit of happiness. They recognized the significance of man's spiritual nature, of his feelings and of his intellect. They knew that only a part of the pain, pleasure and satisfactions of life are to be found in material things. They sought to protect Americans in their beliefs, their thoughts, their emotions and their sensations. They conferred, as against the Government, *the right to be let alone – the most comprehensive of rights and the right most valued by civilized men.*" (emphasis added)

Of course, what Justice Brandeis was referring to was the right to privacy embodied in the Bill of Rights, not the Constitution proper. See also, an analysis by this author of the relationship between privacy and liberty in *Rule By Punch Cards or: How Computers Are a Menace to Liberty*, to be published in 2003 in an anthology about the danger national ID cards pose to the liberty of Americans, available at: www.forejustice.org/ms/rule_by_punch_cards.htm.

[72] At the time Hitler was appointed Chancellor, the German Constitution guaranteed Germans more rights than Americans are under the Bill of Rights to the U.S. Constitution. Among the rights guaranteed Germans were the freedom of the press, free expression of opinion, individual property rights, right of assembly and association, right to privacy of postal and electronic communications, states' rights of self-government, and protection against unlawful searches and seizures. After the Reichstag fire, these rights were suspended on February 28, 1933 by President Paul Von Hindenberg's *Decree of the Reich President for the Protection of the People and State*. This provision is mimicked in the UPACT, that permits Americans to be confined indefinitely without access to a lawyer on the mere suspicion they are involved in terrorist activity or are an enemy combatant.

[73] After the Reichstag Fire, on February 28, 1933 President Hindenberg suspended enforcement of the German Constitutions multitude of individual rights guarantees by invoking Article 48's National Emergency provision. That is mimicked by the effect on Americans labeled as enemy combatants or terrorists or terrorist sympathizers under the Patriot Act.

[74] According to perhaps the most authoritative analysis of mass murder in the 20th Century, Professor Rummel estimated that 43 million people were killed during the reign of Stalin. That is more than double the 21 million that Professor Rummel estimates were killed during the 12 years the National Socialist Workers Party controlled the German government. See: *Death By Government*, R. J. Rummel, New

    A Historical Perspective of How September 11th Has Been Used To Undermine The Liberty of Americans

Brunswick, N.J., Transaction Publishers, 1994. See Professor Rummel's website at: http://www.hawaii.edu/powerkills/welcome.html .

See Appendix B for Chapter X – Fundamental Rights and Duties of Citizens in Constitution of the USSR (Adopted December 1936).

[75] "Camps for Citizens: Ashcroft's Hellish Vision: Attorney general shows himself as a menace to liberty," Jonathan Turley, *Los Angeles Times*, August 14, 2002, B11. The opening two paragraphs are:

> "Atty. Gen. John Ashcroft's announced desire for camps for U.S. citizens he deems to be "enemy combatants" has moved him from merely being a political embarrassment to being a constitutional menace.
>
> Ashcroft's plan, disclosed last week but little publicized would allow him to order the indefinite incarceration of U.S. citizens and summarily strip them of their constitutional rights and access to the courts by declaring them enemy combatants."

[76] One of Henry Kissinger's functions as head of the Commission investigating September 11th is to create a report that will justify a perpetual war against illusory foreign terrorism. That will provide the cover necessary to justify the U.S. military's presence around the world. This harkens to Orwell's *1984* in which each of the three super-powers portrayed each other as the boogeyman – since a powerful enemy was necessary to solidify their domestic power, sustain support for draconian domestic laws, and justify a large standing military force.

IX

Who Benefited From the Events Of September 11, 2001?

When considering that the events of September 11, 2001 were not foreign terrorism, the natural question to ask is: what were they? A key to answering that question is who stood to benefit from those events, who stood to benefit from them being falsely described as acts of foreign terrorism, and who has in fact benefited from them.

Neither al-Qaeda, Iraq, nor any other foreign organization or country meets the criteria of being a beneficiary, which is consistent with the fact that those events were not acts of foreign terrorism.

It is very telling, however, that three domestic groups perfectly meet those three criteria. Those are politicians, federal agencies, and private defense and security oriented companies. The President, and the vast majority of Senators, Representatives and other politicians have not missed an opportunity to capitalize on the events of September 11th to increase their public visibility and boost their poll numbers. Federal agencies such as the FBI, Customs, INS and the IRS have benefited from those events by an increase in the scope of their police powers and/or sphere of authority. While defense contractors are benefiting from the hundreds of billions of dollars in increased military spending attributable to those events, and security companies are in line to benefit from the tens of billons to be spent on security within the U.S. and government facilities outside the U.S.[77]

None of those three groups would have benefited to anywhere near the same degree, if at all from September 11th, if those events had not been characterized as acts of foreign terrorism. Integral with the careful cultivation of that enormous lie has been an unleashing of federal power and the projected expenditure of hundreds of billions to allegedly prevent their reoccurrence. Thus the drumbeaters promoting September 11th as acts of foreign terrorism are not disinterested patriots, but financially, politically and/or professionally self-interested parties. They are the proponents, beneficiaries and/or active participants in the carefully orchestrated effort to construct and profit from an atmosphere of "terror" in this country built on the ashes of September 11th, and the bodies of its innocent victims.

Among those in the media exposing the political and financial underpinnings of the Bush administration's self-proclaimed war on terrorism

– which would have no legs to stand on without being supported by the events of September 11th – is nationally syndicated columnist Sean Gonsalves. One of many examples of Mr. Gonsalves' fine reporting is his summarization in *Connecting the Energy Dots* that the alleged war on terrorism, including all the drum beating about Saddam Hussein and the alleged menace of Iraq to the security of the United States, is driven by politicians and businessmen seeking to respectively maximize their popularity and profits from the deaths and maiming of innocent Americans on September 11th.[78]

An understandable reaction of people to the events of September 11th was shock that they occurred, horror at the devastation, sadness for the people on the airplanes and in the buildings who died or were injured, and sympathy for their family members and friends.

However, September 11th would have faded from the daily consciousness of most Americans if the print and broadcast media had not gone along with the desire of politicians, government officials and business people to ghoulishly use those tragic events as a public relations vehicle to respectively benefit by boosting their popularity, legislated powers and profitability.

Regardless of any other considerations, there is no speculation involved in recognizing that the federal government and those people, organizations and companies associated with it have been the most conspicuous beneficiaries of what occurred on September 11th. Furthermore, those same parties have done *everything* possible to maximize their benefits by using the destruction of the World Trade Centers as the focal point to create an artificial atmosphere of terror in the U.S.

---

[77] See e.g., "The Security Traders: As Washington prepares to spend tens of billions of dollars on homeland security, companies are gearing up for the biggest government bonanza since the Cold War," by Brendan I. Koerner, *Mother Jones*, September/October 2002. Available at,
http://www.motherjones.com/news/feature/2002/37/ma_106_01.html

[78] "Connecting the Energy Dots," Sean Gonsalves, *Cape Code Times*, September 3, 2002. Available at,
http://www.alternet.org/mobile/story_mobile.html?StoryID=14047

X

The Terrorism After September 11th

Although the events used to justify the extreme actions taken by the federal government since September 11, 2001 were not the acts of foreign terrorism that politicians, government officials, and the mass media in this country have portrayed them as being, that doesn't mean they didn't spawn terrorism against Americans, or that they weren't acts of domestic terrorism.

We know by looking to the origin of the word *terrorism* that it came into being during the French Revolution to describe the terror created by the government to intimidate the French people into complying with its edicts. The etymology of *terrorism* is explained in the *Dictionary of Word Origins*: "*Terrorism* and *terrorist* were coined in French in the 1790s to denote the activities of the Revolutionary government during the 'Terror,' when thousands of its opponents were put to death."[79] Correspondingly, a *terrorist* etymologically originated as one who aids the government in its campaign of terrorism against people considered to be a domestic menace to its rule.

As the single most authoritative dictionary one can consult about the meaning of a word in English, the *Oxford English Dictionary* (*OED*) confirms that *terrorism* dates from the 1790s and the French government's systematic campaign of intimidation and terror against people under its rule:

"A system of terror.
Government by intimidation as directed and carried out by the party in power ...
A policy intended to strike with terror those against whom it is adopted; the employment of methods of intimidation;"[80]

The *OED* also recognizes the word *terrorist* likewise dates from the 1790s and the activities of the French government against people in France:

"1. "The terrorists, as they were justly denominated, from the cruel and impolitic maxim of keeping the people in implicit subjection by a merciless severity."
2. One who entertains, professes, or tries to awaken or spread a feeling of terror or alarm; an alarmist, a scaremonger."[81]

In stark contrast to the fact the *OED*'s definition of a terrorist or someone engaging in terrorism against the United States doesn't fit Osama bin Laden, al-Qaeda or any other Islamic group or country, the *OED*'s definition of a terrorist perfectly applies to the conduct of many federal and state politicians, judges and agency officials since September 11th. Those people have diligently worked to create an atmosphere of impending terror from foreigners and insecurity about the ability of the government to prevent or adequately respond to such an event, in order to generate support for the UPACT, the HSA and a general resigning of Americans to their need to abandon the Bill of Rights' symbolic shield against abuses of power by federal agents. Thus, in accord with the OED's definition of terrorism, since September 11th they have "spread a feeling of terror or alarm," and acted as an "alarmist, a scaremonger" to keep "the people in implicit subjection by a merciless severity."[82]

Thus based on the etymological roots of terrorism, it is apparent the extremeness of September 11[ths] events have been used to justify an avalanche of domestic terrorism by the federal government against Americans. Furthermore, politicians and federal agents are the only identifiable terrorists in the U.S. So in spite of being told every day that there is a war on terrorism – it doesn't exist – because the federal government would have to be warring on itself.

Although the major profiteers from the tragic events of September 11th have been politicians, federal agencies and government defense and security contractors, they could not have done so without the active and deliberate complicity of the mass media in deceiving the American people.[83] The staged media events on September 11, 2002 commemorating the events of the previous year can even be classified as terrorism by the federal government against Americans, since the manner in which they were conducted contributed to "spreading a feeling of terror or alarm" about an alleged threat of foreign terrorism.

The 2001 edition of the *New Oxford American Dictionary*, that is a condensed American English version of the *OED*, defines *terrorism* and *terrorist* in a manner consistent with the *Oxford English Dictionary*. Terrorism is defined as "the use of violence and intimidation in the pursuit of political aims." Terrorist is defined as "a person who uses terrorism in the pursuit of political aims."[84]

Those definitions, along with the one's previously cited, support the conclusion federal and state officials have engaged in terrorism since September 11, 2001 by incessantly beating the drum that Americans must be on guard against foreigners wanting to commit acts of terrorism. They have shamelessly used the spectre of that alleged threat to justify a quantum expansion in the invasive presence of the federal government in the lives of Americans – most evidently by enactment of the UPACT and the HSA – even though foreigners did not committed any act of terrorism in this country on September 11th, *nor have they since.*

Furthermore, the federal government has acted consistent with the *OED's* definition of terrorism since September 11th by engaging in various policies "intended to strike with terror those against whom it is adopted; [by] the employment of methods of intimidation." Federal officials such as President Bush and Attorney General Ashcroft have clearly been engaging in efforts to intimidate or cause a feeling of panic in Americans "as a means of affecting political conduct." Those tactics were used to push passage of the UPACT through Congress without a single Congressman or Senator having read its text, they were used to push the federalization of airline screeners through Congress without meaningful debate about its necessity, and those same tactics were also used to push the HSA – the most radical reorganization of the federal government in six decades – through Congress without any Committee hearings, open debate, or any Congressperson studying the Acts provisions, since its text was changed up to the night before it was voted on.

The creation of those circumstances and the intimidating conduct by federal and state officials for political purposes perfectly fits the spectrum of definitions of terrorism engaged in by terrorists set forth in the *Oxford English Dictionary,* the *New Oxford American Dictionary, Merriam-Webster's Dictionary* and *Black's Law Dictionary.* In other words, the terrorism occurring in the United States since September 11th hasn't been by foreigners, but by the federal government.

---

[79] *Dictionary of Word Origins*, John Ayto, Arcade Publishing, NY, 1993 pb ed., p. 525.

[80] *The Oxford English Dictionary*, Vol. XI, T-V, p. 216, 1961 Reprint of 1933 ed. It is noteworthy that the etymology of the word terrorism and the way it is still defined in the OED has an important difference from its definitional tone in the U.S., and one that is *180 degrees* from its meaning in the U.S. The etymological root of terrorism is its linguistic representation of violence and intimidation by a government against the people under its control in the pursuit of promoting its political aims. In contrast, in the U.S. all four classes of definitions (general, legal, statutory and law enforcement as explained in the chapter *How Is Terrorism Defined*) relate to violence and intimidation by people against the government in the pursuit of promoting political aims.

[81] *Id.*

[82] It is important to keep in mind that when analyzed from the perspective of what is in fact a terrorist event (as explained in Chapters IV and V), the two most prominent events prior to September 11th that are typically referred to as caused by terrorists, the 1993 bombing of the World Trade Center and the 1995 bombing of the Murrow Federal Building in Oklahoma City, were *not* terrorist events. It is known that the FBI and the CIA were heavily involved with the people that carried out the WTC bombing in 1993, and the federal agencies had prior knowledge of the planned bombing, including its exact time. Similarly, the BATF had at least two undercover agents within the group in Oklahoma that there is substantial reason to believe was intimately involved in the bombing of the Murrow Federal Building. One of the BATF's undercover agents, Carol Howe, was submitting regular reports to her superiors. Neither of those criminal events that the federal government was integrally involved in was a terrorist event, because neither of them meets the definition of terrorism explained in the Chapters, *How Is Terrorism Defined* and *What Are Acts of Terrorism*.

The involvement of the federal government in the 1993 WTC bombing and 1995's Murrow Federal Building isn't surprising, as its apparent involvement with September 11th isn't surprising. Operation Northwoods was a plan for the U.S. Military to shoot down civilian airliners, destroy civilian ships, stage an attack on U.S. military personnel with mercenaries, and engage in other activities that would be blamed on Fidel Castro, and thus used to justify an invasion of Cuba and the overthrow of his government. President Kennedy's veto of Operation Northwoods, which is subtitled "Justification for U.S. Military Intervention in Cuba," is the only reason it wasn't executed. See copies of Operation Northwoods documents in Appendix A.

[83] The degree of that complicity is exposed in *Into The Buzzsaw: The Myth of a Free Press*, edited by Kristina Borjesson, Prometheus Books, February 2002. *Publisher's Weekly* wrote of the book: "Editor Borjesson succinctly explains the journalist's predicament: "The buzzsaw is what can rip through you when you try to investigate or expose anything this country's large institutions be they corporate or government want kept under wraps.""

[84] *The New Oxford American Dictionary*, Oxford University Press, NY, 2001, p. 1752. The NOAD is Oxford University Press' dictionary of American English that is backed up by its 200 million word data bank of English and the citation files of the OED. It is noteworthy that the NOAD's definitions of terrorism and terrorist bridge the meaning of those words when they came into use during the French Revolution and how they are presently defined in the U.S. The NOAD allows for terrorism and terrorists to be applicable to anyone using violence and intimidation in the promotion of political aims – whether it is used on behalf of the government or in opposition to it. The NOAD's entry for terror also makes that same definitional bridge, although it leans towards violence by the government: "1. extreme fear – the use of such fear to intimidate people, esp. for political reasons. ... (the Terror) the period of the French Revolution between mid 1793 and July 1794 when the ruling Jacobin faction, dominated by Robespierre, ruthlessly executed anyone considered a threat to their regime."

XI

The True Terrorism Of September 11, 2001

Among the plethora of facts consistent with identifying the response by the federal government to the events on September 11 as terroristic, is the acknowledgment by federal officials that there is no known link between any of the nineteen men allegedly involved in the four alleged hijackings on September 11 and al-Qaeda.[85]

Even more remarkably, Thierry Meyssan reveals in *9/11: The Big Lie* that none of the nineteen alleged hijackers was on the passenger manifest of any of the four hijacked airliners, there is no proof that any of them were in fact on any of those airliners, and at least seven of those men are known to have been alive *after* September 11, 2001.[86] One of the alleged dead hijackers, for example, is a very much alive pilot for Royal Air Moroc living in Casablanca. He gave an interview to *Al-Qods, al-Arabi*, a London Arab language daily.[87] Meyssan pulls no punches in describing what those facts mean when contrasted with the official version of September 11th pawned off on the American people by officials of the federal government:

> "To sum things up, the FBI invented a list of hijackers from which it drew an identikit portrait of the enemies of the West. We are asked to believe that these hijackers were Arab Islamic militants who were acting as kamikazes. The domestic American leads were dismissed. In reality, we know nothing, neither the identity of the "terrorists" nor their operational method. All hypotheses remain open. As in all criminal affairs, the first question that should be asked is, "Who profits from the crime?"[88]

As has been explained in previous chapters, including *Who Benefited From the Events of September 11th 2001?*, the beneficiaries have been President Bush, members of Congress, federal agencies, significant campaign contributors (such as drug manufacturers immunized from lawsuits triggered by negative side-effects of their products), and companies catering to the defense department and domestic security needs of the federal government.

Consistent with their efforts to capitalize on the events of September 11 are the numerous reports that federal agencies and high ranking officials, including President Bush, had prior knowledge of what was to occur.[89] Cogent cases have also been made that the federal government actually orchestrated the events.[90] There are compelling but largely ignored reasons pointing directly to the federal government's involvement in the planning and execution of the events on September 11. One of those raises grave concerns in the absence of any others. It is the maxim that *all large scale crimes are inside jobs*: the crimes committed on September 11 were certainly executed on a grand scale. A second reason is the almost too fantastic to be believed fact that *not a single employee or official* at any level of any agency in the federal government was reprimanded as a result of their lack of performance on or prior to September 11th.[91]

The foreign press and investigators have been more conscientious than those in the U.S. at ferreting out and reporting the truth related to what did and did not occur on September 11th.

One of the several books written and published abroad is *9/11: The Big Lie* by French think-tank leader Thierry Meyssan. In that book and a follow-up book *Pentagate*, Meyssan presents the compelling thesis that contrary to popular belief and what is reported in this country, American Airlines Flight 77 did not crash into the Pentagon.[92]

Meyssan's conclusion the purported plane crash didn't occur is supported by a significant body of hard evidence, including numerous photographs of the Pentagon taken after the explosion by surveillance cameras, reporters, private parties and government photographers. The following are just some of the things those photographs clearly reveal:

- The conspicuous absence of debris strewn about from an airliner fuselage, wings, tail, or cabin contents.
- No bodies.
- No jet fuel residue.
- An absence of structural damage to the outside of the Pentagon that a Boeing 757-200 going hundreds of miles an hour would have caused.
- The exit hole in the Pentagon's inner-Ring was at most half the width necessary to accommodate a Boeing airliner.
- The lack of fire damage inside and outside the building that would have been caused by the explosion and burning of many thousands of gallons of jet fuel.

Pentagon surveillance camera photo taken less than 8/1000ths of a second prior to the Pentagon explosion.[93]

The following photo was taken 8/1000ths of a second after the above photo.[94]

A French website called – *Hunt the Boeing* – has many photographs of the Pentagon available for examination that were taken on September 11 and in the days that followed.[95] The website invites viewers to find *any* indication of a Boeing airliner in *any* photograph.

This author spent some weeks looking at every available photograph on the Internet taken of the Pentagon on September 11, 2001 and in the days that followed. He has yet to find a single photograph that supports the government's claim that a Boeing 757-200 crashed into the Pentagon at 9:38am on September 11, 2001.

It is irresponsible and intellectually dishonest not to question the official version of what occurred on September 11th considering the clear and unambiguous photographic evidence Flight 77 did not crash into the Pentagon. The photographs are neutral and would speak for themselves to everyone if not for the mind altering effect of the chorus of voices by those who profited from September 11th that the photos depict something that they don't, and the dissemination of that falsehood by the compliant national news media in the U.S.

Meyssan and others are serving the essential function of simply pointing out the obvious, just like the little boy in *The Emperors New Clothes* did to everyone blinded by uncritically believing the Emperor was wearing clothes that in fact didn't exist except in their imagination.

Photo taken less than five minutes after the Pentagon explosion. This photo clearly shows the absence of any debris, bodies, burning jet fuel, or any other indication a huge Boeing airliner had just crashed into the building.[96]

Meyssan explains that a U.S. military winged missile resembling a small aircraft fits the description of eyewitnesses as to what crashed into the Pentagon. One eyewitness told CNN: "It was like a cruise missile with wings, went right there and slammed into the Pentagon."[97] Another witness working at the Pentagon near the location of the explosion told the *Washington Post*: "We heard what sounded like a missile, then we heard a loud boom."[98]

Consistent with those reports was a hole in the wall of the Pentagon's inner ring at the point of impact that is approximately the width of a defense department missile that resembles a small aircraft.

Tomahawk, a U.S. government missile with wings that resembles a small aircraft

Also supporting the crash of an object much smaller than an airliner into the Pentagon is that minutes after the explosion, Reuters as the first news agency reporting on the explosion, issued a news release that a helicopter had crashed into the Pentagon.[99] The AP confirmed in a news dispatch that the explosion was caused by a small craft.[100] In addition, the Defense Department issued a press release about 20 minutes after the explosion that made no mention the Pentagon was struck by an airplane, much less a huge 115 ton Boeing 757-200 full of fuel like American Airlines Flight 77. Furthermore, the press release made no mention of airline passengers casualties. The announcement, however, did refer to an "attack" that caused casualties to people in the building.[101]

It wasn't until *several hours* after the explosion that a government official publicly floated the idea for the first time that it was attributable to an airliner crash.[102] The absurdity of that claim was revealed during a press conference the next day (September 12, 2001) when the Arlington County, Virginia Fire Marshall acknowledged there was no debris of any kind at the explosion site identifiable as possibly coming from an airplane, except for something that looked like it might be a "nose cone." It is highly unlikely what the Fire Marshall was referring to was in fact the nose cone of whatever struck the Pentagon, because that would be the part most likely to be destroyed upon impact. The Fire Marshall also acknowledged there was no evidence of any of Flight 77's 70,000+ pounds of jet fuel, except for a "small puddle" of some kind of liquid he couldn't readily identify.[103]

Another extremely odd fact is that since a few days after the event at the Pentagon, there has been an eerie silence about it compared to the unending hoopla concerning the airliners that crashed into the World Trade Center towers.[104]

Consistent with Meyssan's thesis that the official version of what caused the explosion at the Pentagon on September 11 is media disseminated government propaganda, are eyewitness accounts and professional opinions that the collapse of the World Trade Center buildings could not have been caused by the airliner that crashed into each one – and that their destruction was caused by pre-planned demolition.

Firemen and other eyewitnesses at the scene who heard explosions at the base of the buildings rejected the official story that the crashes caused the buildings to implode. Likewise, the professional review, *Fire Engineering*, rejected that the airliners caused the buildings to implode after analyzing all the factors related to the crash, including the construction of the buildings, and the heat and distribution of the fire caused by the airliner's fuel.[105] In addition, Van Romero, a world renowned expert from the New Mexico Institute of Mining and Technology, expressed the opinion that only explosives could have caused the implosion of the buildings.[106] The witness testimonials and the analysis of the buildings construction are empirically supported by the fact the buildings were designed to withstand being crashed into by an modern jet airliner without simply falling down like a rickety house of cards.[107]

The federal government's possible behind the scenes role in what transpired on September 11th is empirically supported by a plethora of inconsistencies, circumstantial suspicions and incriminating facts.[108] One of those is that video equipment located at strategic vantage points captured the crashes with crystal clarity from different angles. The supposition that occurred by mere happenstance is not only undermined by the astronomical odds against its happening, but by what might have been a Freudian slip by President Bush when he stated during a citizen meeting in Orlando, Florida on December 4, 2001, that he saw the *first* airliner crash into the *first* World Trade Center building *as it occurred*.[109] He only could have done so if there were pre-positioned television cameras broadcasting the crashes in real time to selective insiders. Additionally, in President Bush's first public announcement, *four hours* after the events on the morning of September 11th, he made no reference whatsoever attributing them to foreign terrorism or that they were caused by foreign terrorists. He merely referred to them one time in five paragraphs as "attacks."[110] Of course, the sheer magnitude of the negligence by the U.S. military and intelligence and highest levels of political authority points directly to complicity in what occurred on

September 11th.[111]

Information in Meyssan's book is complemented to varying degrees by what is disclosed in other books, including, *The War On Freedom* (2002) by Nefeez Mosaddeq Ahmed, and, *Forbidden Truth: U.S.-Taliban Secret Oil Diplomacy, Saudi Arabia and the Failed Search for bin Laden* (2002) by Jean-Charles Brisard, Guillaume Dasquie, and Lucy Rounds.

The volatility of the information in those books is indicated by the manner in which they have been made available in the U.S. Meyssan's book, printed in France, was not released in the U.S. as scheduled on September 11, 2002 because of difficulties clearing Customs, *The War On Freedom* was issued by a small specialty publisher in the U.S., and the U.S. edition of *Forbidden Truth* is 74 pages less than the edition published in France.[112]

The extraordinary circumstances surrounding many issues related to the events of September 11th not only support the possibility that federal agencies and elected officials had prior knowledge, but lend credence to speculation it was a covert federal operation. There is a growing body of compelling empirical evidence that federal military, intelligence and political officials were behind the planning, execution and cover-up of the events that occurred on September 11th. A significant factor driving investigations by concerned individuals and independent organizations into this aspect of those events is federal agencies and operatives were the only ones possessing the inside knowledge, connections, and human and technological resources necessary to carry out an operation of that scale on U.S. soil. That is consistent with the maxim that all big crimes are inside jobs.

The Washington Times, for example, reported that at least one Senator, Patrick J. Leahy (VT D), has referred to the attacks as avoidable.[113] Another strongly circumstantial factor indicating the federal government's involvement is it is the world's all-time greatest master of perpetrating mass destruction, and it has an unabashed willingness to engage in it under the flimsiest of pretexts. After all, if someone wants to cause serious physical damage and loss of life, the U.S. military and intelligence services supporting its activities are the "go to guys and gals."[114]

Compared to the U.S. military's extraordinarily high level of expertise at causing mass destruction and ready access to resources able to do so like missiles, planes, ships, tanks, etc., Osama bin Laden and al-Qaeda are rank novices. Especially if they tried to covertly do something in a foreign land such as the U.S. where they would stand out due to their different appearance, native language, religion, and customs.

If as it strongly appears, the federal government was actively involved in the financing, planning and execution of what occurred on September 11th, then those events meet both prongs of being definable as acts of terrorism. First, they were acts of "politically motivated violence." Second, they were executed by "subnational groups or clandestine agents."[115]

It is responsible, and indeed a moral imperative for all conscientious Americans to be willing to face the distinct possibility the federal government was intimately involved in September 11th. Particularly considering it is known the U.S. military and intelligence services planned and had every intention of executing a major terrorist operation against Americans in the early 1960s, until President Kennedy vetoed it. Known as Operation Northwoods, it was designed to justify U.S. military intervention in Cuba for the purpose of overthrowing Fidel Castro's government by blaming him for such things as: shooting down civilian airliners with Americans on them; blowing up civilian ships near Cuba with Americans on board; and attacking the U.S. military base at Guantanamo Bay.[116] The planes and ships would have been destroyed by the U.S. military and the ground attack would have been carried out by U.S. paid mercenaries. As it was planned and ready to be executed, thousands of civilians and U.S. military personnel could have died if Operation Northwoods had been permitted to be carried out. The documentation of that operation provides positive proof the U.S. military and intelligence services have no compunction about killing thousands of American citizens and U.S. military personnel in the pursuit of their objectives.[117] They are purely driven by an end justifies the means mentality.

While it is known there was no foreign terrorism related to the events of September 11th, there is substantial and circumstantial evidence that those events were domestic terrorist actions carried out by agencies of the U.S. government against the American people.

---

[85] It is also noteworthy that fifteen of those men were Saudi Arabian – a military ally of the U.S. At a minimum the federal government is engaging in misdirection, which is an indicator that it may eventually come to light that government agent provocateurs were responsible for the events themselves.

[86] *9/11: The Big Lie*, Thierry Meyssan, Carnot Publishing, Paris, FR, Oct 2002, at 54-55. Meyssan's book was published in Europe under the title: *The Frightening Fraud*. In *9/11* Thierry Meyssan reports that five of those men are alive. *The War on Freedom* expands on that by reporting that at least *seven* of the alleged hijackers were known to be alive after September 11, 2001.

[87] *Id.* at 54.

^{88} *Id.* at 56.

^{89} One website that has a considerable amount of information about prior knowledge by federal officials and agencies of September 11ths events is Alex Jones' InfoWars, at: http://www.infowars.com/resources.html.

^{90} Among the numerous books presenting various aspects of the involvement of the U.S. government in the events of September 11, 2001 are: *9/11: The Big Lie*, Thierry Meyssan, Carnot Publishing, Paris, FR, Oct 2002; *The War On Freedom*, Nefeez Mosaddeq Ahmed, Media Messenger Books, Joshua Tree, CA, July 2002; and, *Forbidden Truth: U.S.-Taliban Secret Oil Diplomacy, Saudi Arabia and the Failed Search for bin Laden*, Jean-Charles Brisard, Guillaume Dasquie and Lucy Rounds, Avalon Publishing Group, NY, August 2002.

^{91} In contrast, a senior FBI official was reprimanded after the 1992 events at Ruby Ridge that resulted in the shooting deaths of Vicki Weaver and her son. Also, after the events at Waco, Texas related to the Branch Davidians in 1993, two BATF agents were reprimanded. Although people died during both of those events, they were significantly less in scale to the loss of life and property damage that occurred on September 11, 2001. Yet it has not been publicly reported that a single government employee, official or private contractor has been given even a verbal reprimanded related to their performance, or lack thereof on September 11th.

^{92} *Pentagate*, Thierry Meyssan, Carnot, Paris, FR, 2002. See e.g., *French Book, A Best-Seller, Denies Pentagon Crash*, London (CNSNews.com), at: http://www.townhall.com/news/politics/200204/FOR20020405c.shtml. See also: "Frightening Fraud Continues? Organizers of Sept.11 Tragedy Named," *Pravda* English Version, May 23, 2002, at: http://english.pravda.ru/main/2002/05/23/29196.html.

^{93} Source: http://www.airdisaster.com/photos/aa77/photo.shtml. This is the first in a series of five photos on the Air Disaster.Com website that were taken by a Pentagon Surveillance Camera in the space of 4/100s of a second.

^{94} Source: http://www.airdisaster.com/photos/aa77/photo.shtml.

^{95} *Hunt the Boeing* is the French website with photographs of the Pentagon after the September 11, 2001 explosion. The original website is no longer online (http://www.asile.org/citoyens/numero13/pentagone/erreurs_en.htm). However, it is now available at, http://www.serendipity.li/wot/erreurs_en.htm (last viewed August 1, 2018).

This author spent some weeks looking at every available photograph on the Internet taken of the Pentagon on September 11, 2001 and in the days that followed. He has yet to find a single photograph that supports the government's claim that a Boeing 757-200 crashed into the Pentagon at 9:38am on September 11, 2001.

^{96} Source: http://216.239.53.100/search?q=cache:NUHZ11EicNIC:www.crc-internet.org/june2a.htm+pentagon+meyssan+missile+photo&hl=en&ie=UTF-8. The site states in regards to this picture:

"Emmanuel Ratier published a document on the Internet on 18 October, one month after the attacks. On 21 March, it was in fact to him that Le Monde and Actualité juive gave first prize for this incredible news, illustrated with a series of photographs entitled: No plane crashed into the

Pentagon. As surprises go, it was indeed a surprise! Incredible? One has only to examine the AFP photo, above, to understand that it is the pure and simple truth: it stares one in the face!

The photograph was taken in the first minutes of the fire. Fire trucks are on the scene, but as yet these vehicles have not gone into action. Moreover, the upper floors of the building are yet to collapse. Now, there is no trace of significant debris, no engine, no black box, no undercarriage. Nothing! And yet, according to the official version, a Boeing 757-200, an air freighter with a wingspan of 38.05m, a length of 47.30m, a height of 13m and a weight of 100 tons, struck the ground and first floors of the front of the building, hedge-hopping as it approached, flying just a few metres above the ground at a minimum speed of 400 km per hour, without knocking down a single streetlamp or even causing any damage to the magnificent lawn in the foreground, the car park, or the helipad."

[97] ""It was like a cruise missile with wings, went right there and slammed into the Pentagon," Mike Walter, an eyewitness, told CNN." *Up To 800 Possibly Dead At Pentagon*, CNN News, September 12, 2001, at: http://www.cnn.com/2001/US/09/11/pentagon.terrorism/ .

Complementing that eyewitness report that an airliner did not crash into the Pentagon is the following report of an eyewitness who saw the object that crashed into the Pentagon from a distance of little more than a football field was printed in the afternoon edition of *The Washington Post* on September 11, 2001:

"Steve Patterson, 43, said he was watching television reports of the World Trade Center being hit when he saw a silver commuter jet fly past the window of his 14th-floor apartment in Pentagon City. The plane was about 150 yards away, approaching from the west about 20 feet off the ground, Patterson said.

He said the plane, which sounded like the high-pitched squeal of a fighter jet, flew over Arlington cemetery so low that he thought it was going to land on I-395. He said it was flying so fast that he couldn't read any writing on the side.

The plane, which appeared to hold about eight to 12 people, headed straight for the Pentagon but was flying as if coming in for a landing on a nonexistent runway, Patterson said:

"At first I thought 'Oh my God, there's a plane truly misrouted from National,'" Patterson said. "Then this thing just became part of the Pentagon .,.,. I was watching the World Trade Center go and then this. It was like Oh my God, what's next?""

He said the plane, which approached the Pentagon below treetop level, seemed to be flying normally for a plane coming in for a landing other than going very fast for being so low. Then, he said, he saw the Pentagon "envelope" the plane and bright orange flames shoot out the back of the building." *'Extensive Casualties' in Wake of Pentagon Attack, Barbara Vobejda (staff),* Washington Post, September 11, 2001.

[98] "'Extensive Casualties' in Wake of Pentagon Attack," Barbara Vobejda (staff), *Washington Post*, September 11, 2001.

[99] *9/11: The Big Lie* at 14.

[100] *Id.* at 15. The AP later issued at least one report that the damage was caused by explosives detonated in a truck parked near the Pentagon.

[101] *Id.* at 13.

[102] *Id.* at 15. This announcement was by the newly appointed Joint Chiefs of Staff, General Richard Myers. The absurdity of the hours it took for government officials to settle on the story that Flight 77 crashed into the Pentagon is emphasized by considering one idea. If a huge 115 ton airliner with a fuselage 155 feet long and a wingspan of 125 feet crashed into the largest and most populated building in any major city, is it reasonable to even suggest that minutes after the crash that international and national news agencies would report the object was a relatively small helicopter or some other small object, and then several hours later have those reports contradicted by a government spokesperson claiming the damage was actually caused by a huge commercial airliner crashing into the building? The government's manufactured cover story that Flight 77 crashed into the Pentagon is facially absurd. Of course, the great mystery of Flight 77 is where it crashed. It is reasonable to surmise it crashed into the Atlantic Ocean, since its wreckage would have otherwise been found by now if it had crashed on the mainland U.S.

[103] *Id.* at 23. 70,000 pounds of jet fuel is approx. 10,300 gallons. The capacity of a Boeing 757-200 is a minimum of 11,276 gallons.

[104] The greatest mystery of the new century is what happened to American Airlines Flight 77 and the people that were on it.

[105] *9/11: The Big Lie*, at 35. Meyssan wrote: "This theory was vigorously rejected by the New York firemen's associations and the professional review, *Fire Engineering*, which, backed up by calculations, claimed that the structures could have resisted the fire for a long period. The firemen affirm that they heard explosions at the base of the buildings and demanded the opening of an independent investigation." The cited article is at fn. 23 in Meyssan's book, and it can be found at: "Selling Out The Investigation," by Bill Manning, *Fire Engineering*, January 2002. See also, *WTC Investigation? A Call for Action* (A petition published in the same issue of the review). *Id.* at 215.

[106] *Id.* at 35.

[107] The allegation the heat from the burning jet fuel was the trigger causing the implosion of both buildings has nothing to do with the type of airplane that struck the buildings, and it is contradictory with the fact the buildings were specifically designed to withstand a direct airliner crash – which both buildings did, and the resulting fire – which we have every reason to believe they also did. As noted in a previous footnote, "the professional review, *Fire Engineering*, which, backed up by calculations, claimed that the structures could have resisted the fire for a long period." *Id.* at 35.

[108] One website that has a considerable amount of information about prior knowledge by federal officials and agencies is Alex Jones' InfoWars, at: http://www.infowars.com/resources.html .

[109] For the text of President Bush's statement see: *9/11: The Big Lie*, at 37-38. An audio recording of President Bush's admission is at: www.forejustice.org/audio/george_bush_admitting_he_saw_wtc.mp3

[110] *Id.* at 46-47. This was released to the public at 1:04 pm East Coast time. In addition, during two press briefings by Presidential Spokesperson Ari Fleischer on September 11th, he did make any reference to the "attacks" as being foreign terrorism, or that foreign terrorists were believed to be involved. *Id.* at 47.

[111] In *The War On Freedom* by Nefeez Mosaddeq Ahmed, Media Messenger Books, Joshua Tree, CA, 2002, some of the negligence by these agencies and officials is explained in the section titled: *Myers and Bush on 9/11: Negligence Points to Complicity*, at pp. 159-166.

[112] This author was told by a representative of Carnot Publishing that the release of *9/11: The Big Lie* was delayed for six weeks until late October 2002, due to difficulties with the book, that is printed in France, clearing U.S. Customs. This interference by U.S. Customs caused the publisher to lose the momentum generated by the nationwide buzz and publicity buildup about the book, including the following mention in the NY Times: "…challenges the entire official version of the September 11th attacks." (cover of *9/11: The Big Lie*).

[113] "September 11 Attacks Called Avoidable," Joyce Howard Price, *The Washington Times*, June 9, 2002. Senator Leahy was quoted as saying: "There was plenty of information available before September 11. I think historians are going to find, tragically, that, had it been acted upon, the hijackers could have been stopped," Available at: http://www.washtimes.com/national/20020609-22093908.htm

[114] As the most militaristically adventurous country in the world since WWII, the U.S. is generally viewed by people of most, and perhaps all other countries as the savage and barbarous "Big Bad U.S." In *Nuremberg and Vietnam*, for example, Telford Taylor, the Allies chief prosecutor at the Nuremberg trials after WWII, explains how the U.S. military's normal tactics of warfare turned the Vietnamese people at the grassroots level against the U.S. In other words, the Vietnamese people viewed the United States as foreign invaders and not liberators. [Source: *Nuremberg and Vietnam: an American Tragedy*, Telford Taylor, Bantam, NY, 1970, Chapter 8 – War and Peace, pp. 183-207, esp. 195-207] On August 2, 1970 for example, The New York Times published reporter Gloria Emerson's first hand report under the headline, *Americans in Vietnam Find Themselves Hated*. [Source: *Id.* at 195-196, fn. 16.] If foreign terrorism ever does come to the U.S., it will be the chickens coming home to roost and a self-fulfillment of the prophecy that it is bound to happen sooner or later, since the U.S. government has actively engaged in foreign terrorism for over 160 years. The U.S. is known to have invaded foreign countries over 200 times for the express purpose of influencing the internal politics of those countries.

[115] 22 U.S.C. §2656f(d)(2). For a full explanation see the chapter, *How Is Terrorism Defined?*

[116] See Appendix A for photocopies of Operation Northwoods documents. The operation included many more nefarious activities than the few significant ones explained in this book. See also *9/11: The Big Lie* at 198-205.

[117] *Id.*

XII
Final Words

The events of September 11, 2001 were not acts of foreign terrorism. That simple fact is apparent from understanding the common definitions of the word terrorism. Furthermore, no event of any kind has occurred in the U.S. since then that can be described as foreign terrorism. So there is no substantiation for the federal government to implement measures to counter non-existent foreign terrorist events.

On September 11, 2001 terrorism was defined *generally, legally, statutorily* and by *law enforcement* agencies as an action involving two prongs: 1) an action intended to affect political policies, 2) by people associated with a group. Neither the nineteen alleged hijackers, Osama bin Laden and al-Qaeda, nor *any* known Islamic group or country meets the first prong – because none of them exerted any pressure or made any political demands on the U.S. government related to the events of September 11th. Consequently, the events of September 11th do not meet any of the four different types of definitions describing what could be considered an act of foreign terrorism. Which means that even if it were eventually proven that Osama bin Laden and al-Qaeda, or any other foreign group or country was involved in September 11th, they could only be alleged to have committed crimes.

There is simply no definitional basis to legitimately characterize the events of September 11th as foreign terrorism. The well orchestrated multi-pronged political and media campaign to do so is one of the greatest frauds ever attempted by a government in the history of the world.

Although the acts themselves weren't foreign terrorism, that doesn't mean there hasn't been terrorism related to September 11th. The Oxford English Dictionary clearly shows that *beginning minutes after the first event on September 11th*, the actions of innumerable federal and state politicians and agencies perfectly met the definition of people and groups engaging in terrorist activities in the promotion of terrorism against the American people. Those people and organizations associated with federal and state governments began working overtime to "spread a feeling of terror or alarm," in order to influence the thinking of Americans, judges and reluctant public officials about proposed legislation, and the way that existing legislation should be executed.

The etymological roots of terrorism reveal the federal governments is engaging in terrorism by using the events of September 11th to encourage a feeling of terror and apprehension in Americans about their safety as a device to generate support for its political policies, legislative agenda and further distance itself from the Americans under its control. It can even be said that the events sponsored by the federal government commemorating the first anniversary of those events were terrorism, since they were used as a platform to continue spreading "a feeling of terror or alarm." The federal government's systematic response to September 11th has been to maximize support for political policies that would otherwise have insufficient backing to be seriously considered, much less enacted, in the absence of those events. The most visible of those are the Patriot Act, and the Homeland Security Act, but they also include such things as the federalization of airport screeners, the federalization of insurance claims related to losses resulting from events labeled as terrorist, and creation of the Defense Departments Information Assurance Office.[118]

Consequently, September 11th has been used to enact legislation that can not be characterized as having even a superficial relationship to combating foreign terrorism – which is consistent with the fact that is not what they were.

Thus at a minimum, the true terrorism attributable to September 11th has been the after the fact response by federal politicians and officials. That after the fact domestic terrorism is compounded by possible involvement of the federal government in the events themselves. The manner in which the federal government has sought to maximize its benefits from the tragic events of September 11th would raise grave suspicions of its possible complicity in them in the absence of any other indications of its involvement.

Those events, regardless of whether the federal government was intimately involved with their financing, planning and/or execution, were criminal acts, and their perpetrators are prosecutable under existing laws. If for some reason a person chose not to call them what they were – criminal acts – then English imposes no impediment to the immediate creation of a new word if none of its estimated 500,000+ words is considered adequate at expressing what a person considers those actions to have been.

The mischaracterization of what occurred on September 11th as foreign terrorism obscures that existing criminal laws provide as much justice for the survivors of those events, and as much protection for society, as can be expected from the prosecution, trial and punishment of any person that commits any horrible crime. Stated as plainly as possible, that means neither the UPACT nor the HSA, nor the federalization of airport security screeners, nor any other action by the federal government since September 11th has any relationship to preventing a reoccurrence of those events or finding its perpetrators.

Given the degree of disinformation dispensed by the federal government about the Pentagon explosion, and the circumstances of the planes that crashed into the twin WTC towers and their subsequent collapse, the disassociation between the concern for preventing a reoccurrence of those events and the UPACT and the HSA is predictable. The dissemination of disinformation about the events of September 11th by the media is predictable considering the federal government's penchant for dispensing untruthful information to domestic and foreign media sources.[119]

Since September 11th the federal government has relied on the principle of political policy attributed to Adolf Hitler: "The great masses of the people... will more easily fall victims to a big lie than to a small one." Yet not even the Nazi's attempted to foist a lie on the German people as mammoth as the federal government's preposterous tale that a Boeing 757-200 crashed into the Pentagon at 9:38 am on September 11, 2001.

Convincing many tens of millions of people to accept the myth that the events of September 11, 2001 were foreign terrorism has depended on bastardization of the English language that George Orwell warned about in his 1945 essay, *Politics and the English Language*. As would be expected from employment of such tactics of gross deception, the perpetration of that fantasy has done nothing to improve the lives of Americans, while it has harmed them in a number of ways. Not the least of which is the incessant domestic terrorism innocent and decent Americans have been subjected to by federally employed and associated terrorists. They are getting away with doing so in broad daylight without any significant opposition by throwing the 'spectre of terrorism card' on the table at every opportunity as a way to both silence intelligent inquiry, and to justify imposition of draconian legislation and policies without meaningful debate. Those government terrorists, from the President on down, are taking advantage of September 11th to invade the privacy of Americans and enact legislation opening the floodgates to restrictions on their liberty and impairing application of their protections from the federal government under the Bill of Rights.

Consequently, the illusions foisted on Americans by the federal government concerning September 11th have neither increased their health, welfare or security, nor can they. What the myth of foreign terrorism has done is provide essential support for actions by the federal government that amount to nothing less than a de facto declaration of war by the United States government against America and the American people.

The grave threat to the liberty of Americans is not from the menace of terrorists from without the country, but by the federal government and its cadre of terrorists within this country.

---

[118] For an analysis by the National Taxpayer's Union of the federalization of insurance losses attributable to terrorist acts, see:
http://www.ntu.org/features/ntu_on_capitolhill/T0110KeatingTerrorInsuranc.php3.
[119] An example of this is *The New York Times* reported on February 19, 2002 the Pentagon's Office of Strategic Influence is "developing plans to provide news items, possibly even false ones, to foreign media organizations" in an effort "to influence public sentiment and policy makers in both friendly and unfriendly countries." See: http://www.fair.org/activism/osi-propaganda.html.

Additional Chapters

The following are chapters added to the original 2002 edition.

XIII

Usama Bin Laden Was Not Responsible For 9/11

One of the most persistent myths regarding 9/11 is Usama (Osama) bin Laden was responsible. Yet, bin Laden was never indicted by the U.S. government for 9/11, and he not only never publicly stated he and/or al-Qaeda was involved, but he repeatedly publicly denied involvement.

The FBI's biographical webpage for Usama (Osama) bin Laden does not contain a single word regarding 9/11:

Usama (Osama) Bin Laden

Usama (or Osama) Bin Laden, founder of the al-Qaeda terrorist organization, was born in Saudi Arabia in 1957. On March 10, 1984, Bin Laden and others killed two German nationals. On March 16, 1998, authorities in Tripoli issued an arrest warrant for him for murder and illegal possession of firearms. Bin Laden was also wanted for the August 1998 bombing of U.S. embassies in Kenya and Tanzania. He was killed by U.S. forces in May 2011.[1]

There is no credible evidence that Usama bin Laden and al-Qaeda had anything to do with 9/11. That is consistent with bin Laden's statement six days after 9/11 disclaiming any involvement with those days events:

"I would like to assure the world that I did not plan the recent attacks, which seems to have been planned by people for personal reasons. I have been living in the Islamic emirate of Afghanistan and following its leaders' rules. The current leader does not allow me to exercise such operations."[2]

He followed that up about ten days later with an interview in which he elaborated on his September 17 disclaimer:

"I have already said that I am not involved in the 11 September attacks in the United States. As a Muslim, I try my best to avoid telling a lie. I had no knowledge of these attacks, nor do I consider the killing of innocent women, children and other humans as an appreciable act. Islam strictly forbids causing harm to innocent women, children and other people. Such a practice is forbidden even in the course of a battle."[3]

The following article detailing bin Laden's legal innocence was published by *Justice Denied* on July 1, 2011.[4]

Usama bin Laden Is Legally Innocent:
1993 And 1998 Indictments Are Dismissed

By Hans Sherrer

On June 17, 2011 U.S. District Court Judge Lewis A. Kaplan ordered dismissal of two federal grand jury indictments of Usama bin Laden.[5] The dismissals were in response to a *nolle prosequi* motion filed by the U.S. Attorney's Office in Manhattan based on evidence that bin Laden was killed on May 1, 2011. Usama bin Laden was commonly referred to in the press as Osama bin Laden.

Usama bin Laden aka Osama bin Laden (AP)

The indictments were the only pending criminal charges against bin Laden.

In June 1998 bin Laden was secretly indicted by a federal grand jury in New York City on one count of "Conspiracy to Attack Defense Utilities of the United States."[6] The only act of violence alleged in the indictment (98 CR 539) was:

1. On October 3 and 4, 1993, members of al-Qaeda participated with Somali tribesmen in an attack on United States military personnel serving in Somalia as part of Operation Restore Hope, which attack killed a total of 18 United States soldiers and wounded 73 others in Mogadishu;

After truck bombings in August 1998 outside the U.S. embassies in Dar es Salaam, Tanzania and Nairobi, Kenya killed 224 people, including 12 U.S. citizens, an indictment was issued against bin Laden in November 1998. The indictment (98 CR 1023) alleged among other things that bin Laden conspired to kill Americans for his support of the embassy bombings. That indictment was supplemented by two superseding indictments, the first in June 1999 and the second in May 2000. Those superseding indictments did not add any new acts of violence that bin Laden allegedly supported.

Bin Laden was added on June 7, 1999 to the FBI's Most Ten Wanted list. His FBI poster stated he was wanted for "Murder Of U.S. Nationals Outside The United States, Conspiracy To Murder U.S. Nationals Outside The United States, Attack On A Federal Facility Resulting In Death."[7]

Hours after the events of September 11, 2001 elected officials claimed and the press widely reported that bin Laden was the mastermind. Bin Laden was not bashful about taking credit for the things he was involved in, but he publicly denied any involvement in 9/11. Consistent with bin Laden's denials the United States did not attempt to pursue any criminal terrorism charges against bin Laden related to 9/11 or for any alleged harm to any American anywhere in the world

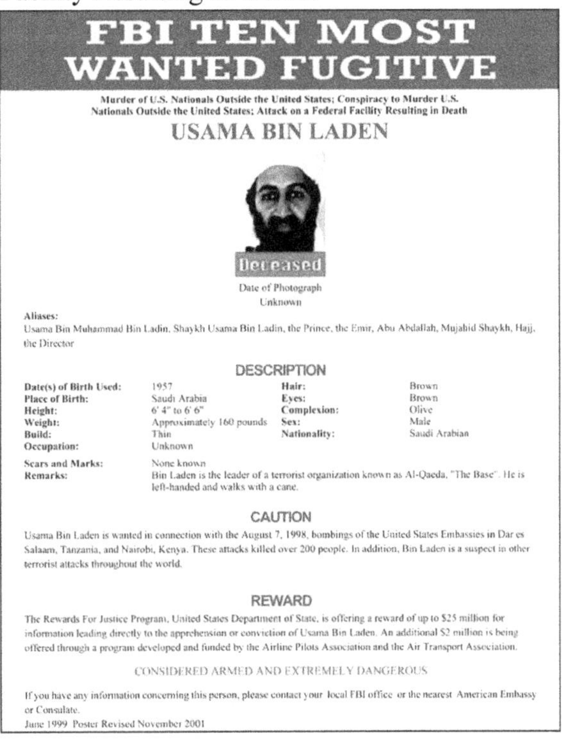

after the August 1998 east African embassy bombings, for which he had been indicted. That fact did not interfere with public officials and the press painting bin Laden for years after 9/11 as a satanic figure with almost supernatural like powers to direct his minions around the world from a secret enclave. Bin Laden was portrayed by politicians and the media as a real-life Emanuel Goldstein – who was the boogeyman in George Orwell's *1984* that the government relied on to justify its repressive domestic policies.

There was speculation in the years following September 11, 2001 that bin Laden was dead, but on May 1, 2011 it was reported that U.S. Navy seals had stormed bin Laden's home in Abbottabad, Pakistan without the fore-knowledge or permission of the Pakistani government and killed him. It has been reported that bin Laden was unarmed and in his bedroom wearing nightclothes at the time he was repeatedly shot. There was no reported attempt to apprehend bin Laden alive. It has also been reported that afterwards bin Laden was buried at sea, and to date no pictures of him related to the May 2011 raid or his burial have been publicly released.[8]

Bin Laden died with no criminal history because he had never been convicted of any crime in the United States or any other country. Bin Laden, a former U.S. government asset and CIA operative, had never even been arrested for an alleged crime. When bin Laden was removed from the FBI's Most Ten Wanted list in May 2011 his FBI poster did not state he was wanted for any alleged criminal act or terrorism committed in the United States, or anywhere in the world after the 1998 embassy bombings.

The circumstances of Bin Laden's death that have been reported are disturbing to Americans because he was under indictment by the U.S. government for alleged criminal acts against Americans in foreign countries in 1993 and 1998. The United States Department of State offered a reward of up to $25 million for information leading directly to the apprehension or conviction of Usama Bin Laden. Bin Laden was officially classified as a fugitive from justice, and his extradition could have been sought from a country where he was captured.

It is known that when convenient the U.S. government has bypassed the extradition process and kidnapped a person for return to the U.S. for trial. A well-known case is that of Panama's Manuel Noriega. As the head of Panama Defense Forces Noriega was the *de facto* ruler of Panama from 1983 to Jan. 1990. Noriega was a valuable ally of President Ronald Reagan in the fight against Communist influence in Central America. After Reagan left office Noriega was federally indicted in the U.S. for drug trafficking, racketeering, and money laundering charges. The U.S. military invaded Panama on December 20, 1989.[9] On December 29, the United Nations General Assembly voted, 75–20 (with 40 abstentions) to condemn the U.S. invasion as a "flagrant violation of international law."[10] Noriega was forcibly transported to the United States following his capture on January 3, 1990.[11] Noriega was convicted by a jury in April 1992 of all charges and sentenced to 40 years in federal prison.[12] His sentence that was reduced to 30 years on appeal, was completed in 2007. Noriega was held in custody for almost three years fighting extradition to France. In April 2010 Noriega was extradited to France, where he was convicted of money laundering in July 2010 and sentenced to seven years in prison.[13]

Noriega's case illustrates that every person accused of a federal crime – regardless of who they are, where they are, or what they allegedly did or didn't do – has specific due process rights, including the right to a jury trial to ascertain the truthfulness of the charges against him or her.

                    Usama Bin Laden Was Not Responsible For 9/11

The invasion of bin Laden's home in the middle of the night without a warrant and the summary shooting of him when he was unarmed has no precedent in American history as an action that conforms with the accepted norm of due process. Under the common-law dating back to the Magna Carta in 1215 a person's home is their castle and a person has the right to forcibly resist an unlawful invasion of his or her home by authorities.[14] The federal government made no effort to lawfully search bin Laden's home under U.S. or Pakistani law, and there has been no evidence publicly disclosed that the military personnel involved even had an arrest warrant for bin Laden -- or that he forcibly resisted arrest. When you strip away the hysterical rhetoric about bin Laden the pre-planned storming of his home without any judicial process is no more legally justifiable than the police using lethal force against an unarmed person whose home is stormed without warning and without a warrant in Evansville, Indiana or Bakersfield, California.[15] That is particularly the case in a situation such as bin Laden's when there was not even an allegation that he had ever personally killed anyone.[16]

In contrast with bin Laden's treatment, was that of former Boston mobster and FBI informant Whitey Bulger. Bulger was on the FBI's Most Wanted List for allegedly personally committing more than a dozen murders. In spite of being a notoriously violent person he was peacefully captured in Santa Monica, California six weeks after bin Laden's home was stormed.[17]

The test of whether due process is an immutable principle or merely something to be given lip service when it is convenient is if it is accorded to a person under the most extreme circumstances. Everyone wants due process to be accorded a respected person accused of a crime, but those same people should just as enthusiastically advocate that an accused serial rapist or murderer must be accorded the same due process rights. If only persons considered respectable are automatically accorded due process, then it is not a right, but a privilege bestowed by the government that can be denied at the discretion of those people in a position of power to do so.

Lynching is decried because it relies on passion and the impression a person is guilty rather than a careful consideration of the facts. Members of a lynch mob fervently feel a person is guilty – and to them that feeling is enough. It is precisely that attitude of blind vigilantism that due process is intended to counter by providing for an analysis of the facts supporting whatever a person is accused of committing.

The lynching of bin Laden by shooting instead of a rope constitutes a triumph of the mob led by President Barack Obama and the major media. It constitutes a breakdown in the rule of law and a public and orderly process to determine if he was guilty of what he was indicted of committing.

After World War II high ranking Nazi officials who had been demonized in the press for years, and who were accused of heinous crimes against humanity light-years beyond anything alleged against bin Laden, were not summarily executed when found or after they were taken into custody. Those persons that included Hitler's right-hand man Hermann Goering, were afforded the due process of public trials during which they had the opportunity to present a vigorous defense to refute the grave charges against them. Only a handful of the high-ranking Nazis were sentenced to death after their conviction, with others receiving a prison term. Some of them were acquitted. Japanese military and civilian officials captured after WWII were also afforded public trials for their alleged crimes.

Prosecutors control the secret grand jury process since they dictate what evidence the grand jurors see and what witnesses testify. That is why it has often been said that a prosecutor can indict a ham sandwich. Consequently an indictment against a person means nothing if the truthfulness of the government's alleged evidence is untested during a public trial.

Although it may seem a novel thought, it is possible that the federal prosecutors' actual evidence against bin Laden for the 1993 and 1998 bombings was so sketchy that he could have been acquitted or had a hung jury after a public trial in the U.S. However, in spite of being legally presumed innocent bin Laden was accorded no due process rights. The possibility he wouldn't have been convicted was eliminated when he was killed with no attempt to apprehend him for a public trial in the U.S. Consequently, bin Laden's death not only denied him his day in court, but it relieved federal prosecutors of ever having a jury judge the value of their evidence in support of his indictments.

Usama bin Laden is legally innocent of ever having violated any state or federal law. Dismissal of his 1993 and 1998 indictments on June 17, 2011 means those indictment's allegations will forever remain unproven accusations. Since he was not indicted for any of the events that occurred on September 11, 2001, there are only sketchy suggestions he was involved in those events.

---

[1] "Usama (or Osama) Bin Laden," FBI Records: The Vault, *The Federal Bureau of Investigation,* https://vault.fbi.gov/osama-bin-laden (last viewed May 1, 2018)
[2] "Bin Laden says he wasn't behind attacks," *CNN.com,* September 17, 2001 http://edition.cnn.com/2001/US/09/16/inv.binladen.denial/ . (Last viewed May 1,

                    Usama Bin Laden Was Not Responsible For 9/11

2018)

3 'Bin-Ladin Denies Involvement in the 9/11 Attacks', By Ummat, (Urdu-language daily newspaper based in Karachi, Pakistan), 9-28-2001, http://911review.com/articles/usamah/khilafah.html . (Last viewed May 1, 2018)

4 The article is online at, http://justicedenied.org/wordpress/archives/1285. The article was published *Justice Denied – the magazine for the wrongly convicted*, Issue 55 (Fall 2013), online at, http://justicedenied.org/issue/issue_55/bin_laden_dismissal_jd55.pdf . (Last viewed May 1, 2018)

5 *USA v Usama bin Laden*, 98 CR 539 and 1023, USDC SD NY (nolle prosequi motion to dismiss indictments), 6-17-2011, http://www.nylj.com/nylawyer/adgifs/decisions/062011binladen.pdf (Last viewed June 28, 2011).

6 June 1998 indictment of Usama bin Laden, http://www.fas.org/irp/news/1998/11/indict1.pdf (Last viewed May 1, 2018).

7 FBI's bin Laden wanted poster was first released in June 1999, and revised in Nov. 2001, http://www.fbi.gov/wanted/topten/usama-bin-laden/view (Last viewed June 28, 2011).

8 There is speculation that bin Laden was not present or killed during the raid on May 1, 2011 given the circumstances that there was no effort to apprehend "bin Laden" alive, and since "his" body was disposed at sea there is no way to independently determine the body's identity. Reports that DNA from the disposed body establish to a high degree of certainty that it was bin Laden are unverifiable because the federal government controls all the evidence, so there is no way to verify that the DNA tested was from the body and not from a bin Laden relative -- or if the DNA test results were not simply fabricated from thin air. Likewise, the technology is readily available to edit a photograph or produce the photograph of a person at a particular place and time -- so the photographs of bin Laden's body that have not yet been publicly released are meaningless without independent verification of his identify from examination of the body. Questions about whether bin Laden died on May 1, 2011 or some time prior to then will persist for decades if not centuries -- just as questions of whether Marilyn Monroe's death was accidental or a murder persist, and there are questions of whether there was a shooter of President Kennedy on the grassy knoll.

9 "Manuel Noriega Fast Facts," *CNN Library*, May 30, 2017, https://www.cnn.com/2013/08/19/world/americas/manuel-noriega-fast-facts/index.html (Last viewed May 1, 2018).

10 "After Noriega: United Nations; Deal Is Reached at U.N. on Panama Seat as Invasion Is Condemned," *The New York Times*, December 30, 1989, https://www.nytimes.com/1989/12/30/world/after-noriega-united-nations-deal-reached-un-panama-seat-invasion-condemned.html?pagewanted=1 (Last viewed May 1, 2018).

11 "Manuel Noriega Fast Facts," *CNN Library*, May 30, 2017, https://www.cnn.com/2013/08/19/world/americas/manuel-noriega-fast-facts/index.html (Last viewed May 1, 2018).

[12] *Id.*

[13] *Id.*

[14] The English common-law right to resist unlawful police action has been traced by scholars to the Magna Carta in 1215. See e.g., Craig Hemmens & Daniel Levin, *Not a Law at All: A Call for the Return to the Common Law Right to Resist Unlawful Arrest*, 29 Sw. U. L. Rev. 1, 9 (1999). In the case of *Bad Elk v. United States*, 177 U.S. 529, 535 (1900) the United States Supreme Court recognized that: "If the officer had no right to arrest, the other party might resist the illegal attempt to arrest him, using no more force than was absolutely necessary to repel the assault constituting the attempt to arrest." The Supreme Court affirmed that right in the 1948 case of *United States v. Di Re*, 332 U.S. 581, 594 (1948) ("One has an undoubted right to resist an unlawful arrest, and courts will uphold the right of resistance in proper cases.").

[15] The case for President George W. Bush's criminal liability for the U.S.'s 2003 invasion of Iraq is detailed in *The Prosecution of George W. Bush for Murder* (Vanguard Press, 2008) by former Los Angeles County Assistant District Attorney Vincent Bugliosi. Bugliosi was the lead prosecutor of Charles Manson and other high-profile defendant. A case can likewise be made that President Obama can bear criminal liability for his executive order that authorized the storming of bin Laden's home during which he was summarily killed. A president cannot at will issue an order that abrogates or otherwise suspends the U. S. Constitution and an indicted person's right to due process of law – especially since a person is legally presumed innocent of the their indicted crime(s) until a jury (or a judge in a bench trial) determines the person has been proven guilty beyond a reasonable doubt in a court of law. For all practical purposes President Obama acted as bin Laden's judge, jury and executioner by issuing his executive order authorizing the raid.

[16] Not only was there no evidence bin Laden was personally violent, but documents seized during the raid on bin Laden's home reveal he was completely marginalized by al-Qaeda's leaders and he had no influence over the organization. A U.S. official description of bin Laden's relationship to al-Qaeda is, "He was like the cranky, old uncle that people weren't listening to." (See, "Official Bin Laden lost influence, was 'cranky, old uncle.'" *The Seattle Times*, June 29, 2011, p. A1, A6.)

[17] "Mobster 'Whitey' Bulger captured in California," By The Associated Press and Los Angeles Times, *The Seattle Times*, June 22, 2011.

XIV

No One Has Credibly Taken Credit For 9/11

Seventeen years after 9/11 no one has credibly taken credit for it. The media has repeated the mantra that Usama bin Laden was responsible millions of times without credible evidence that would stand up as convincing in a criminal case.

The fog obscuring that simple truth is so thick that Wikipedia.org has a page titled "2004 Osama bin Laden video" that claims: "in this video, he accepts responsibility for the September 11 attacks."[1] The problem is that is a fabricated claim. He doesn't accept responsibility in the video. But with that lie repeated untold millions of times a large number of people believe it instead of reality.

It is not by accident that bin Laden was not indicted for 9/11 as explained in the previous chapter: There is no credible evidence he was involved.

Several al-Qaeda members have been criminally charged with knowledge or some degree of involvement in 9/11.[2] That doesn't change that al-Qaeda did not take credit for it. That cannot be surprising because as early as September 23, 2001, the *Washington Post* reported that investigators had not found any connection between al-Qaeda groups in the U.S. and the events on September 11. According to the story, the CIA and the FBI had been tracking al-Qaeda "cells" inside the U.S. for several years and characterized their activities as "possibly benign."[3]

---

[1] "2004 Osama bin Laden video," *Wikipedia: The Free Encyclopedia,* https://en.wikipedia.org/wiki/2004_Osama_bin_Laden_video (last viewed Aug. 1, 2018).

[2] Five of those men are being held by the U.S. military in Guantanamo Bay, Cuba. "Trials related to the September 11 attacks," *Wikipedia: The Free Encyclopedia,* https://en.wikipedia.org/wiki/Trials_related_to_the_September_11_attacks (last viewed Aug. 1, 2018).

[3] "Investigators Identify 4 to 5 Groups Linked to Bin Laden Operating in U.S.," By Bob Woodward and Walter Pincus, *The Washington Post,* September 23, 2001 https://www.washingtonpost.com/archive/politics/2001/09/23/investigators-identify-4-to-5-groups-linked-to-bin-laden-operating-in-us/c568d1e3-4a7c-451a-a8c6-124f3364aad8/?noredirect=on&utm_term=.1a626656def4 (last viewed Aug. 1, 2018).

XV

Malaysian Flight 370 Has Not Been Found

Malaysian Airline Flight MH370 disappeared shortly after midnight on March 8, 2014.[1] The Boeing 777-200 had 239 people on board when it vanished from air traffic control radar about 40 minutes after takeoff from Kuala Lumpur, Malaysia bound for Beijing, China.

No distress signal or message was sent by the plane. The last words received from the plane was the pilot saying "good night Malaysian three seven zero."[2]

Malaysian Flight 370 (Alamy)

Malaysian military radar that tracked the plane for another hour identified it went off course and headed westward 200 miles northwest of Penang Island in northwestern Malaysia before going out of radar range.

Based on that information the search initially focused on the South China Sea.

However, the search area changed when analysis of satellite communications with electronic equipment on the aircraft indicated it had turned south. It was tracked flying for several hours flying over the southern Indian Ocean before contact was lost. The plane had enough fuel to fly for about seven hours. It was presumed to have crashed in the Indian Ocean when it ran out.

The governments of Australia, Malaysia and China spearheaded the most extensive search in aviation history. On March 30, 2014 the Australian government established the Joint Agency Coordination Centre (JACC) to coordinate search and recovery operations for MH370.[3]

Based on analysis of the available data the search focused on a long area south of Malaysia and west of Australia. A surface search covered 1,700,000 square miles of ocean, and an underwater search covered 46,000 square miles.[4]

In July 2015 a small amount of debris believed to be from the plane washed up on an island in the Indian Ocean, close to Madagascar.[5] That is about 4,000 miles west of Malaysia.

There were several ideas publicly discussed about what happened to cause MH370 to go off its flight plan. The idea given the most credibility is pilot sabotage, based on the plane deliberately changing course.[6] That would mean either the co-pilot was in on the plot or the pilot killed or disabled him. The other scenario accounting for the course changes would be hijacking of the plane.

In January 2017 the JACC called off the official search after failing to find anything related to the plane in the area where it was believed to have crashed.[7]

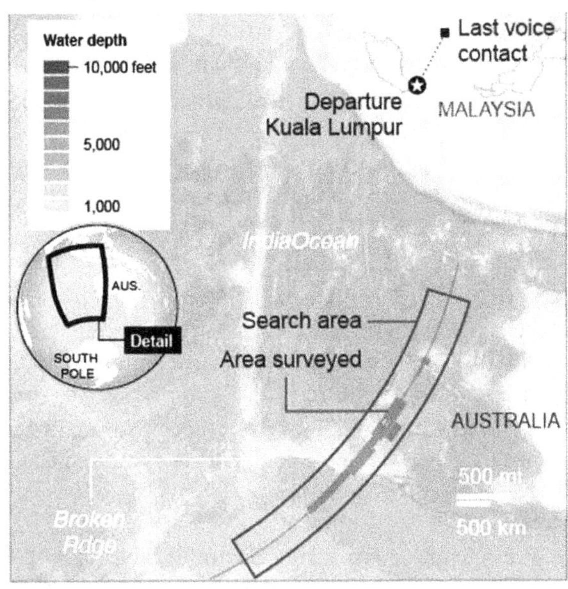

SOURCE: Australian Transport Safety Bureau   AP

In response to criticism for ending the search, in January 2018 the Malaysian government signed an agreement with Ocean Infinity. The private company agreed to conduct a 90-day underwater search for the plane without payment, but if it had found the wreckage or black boxes it would receive a reward of up to $70 million.[8]

On May 28, 2018 Ocean Infinity ended its three-month effort after fruitlessly searching 46,000 square miles of ocean floor.[9]

The final Safety Investigation Report about the search was issued on July 2, 2018.[10] The SIR acknowledged the reason for the Boeing 777's disappearance and its exact location is unknown. The Report stated: "Despite an extensive air and sea search, the location of the aircraft and occupants remains unknown."[11] It further stated: "In conclusion, the Team is unable to determine the real cause for the disappearance of MH370."[12]

So the most expensive search in history for an aircraft lost at sea resulted in a failure to find the aircraft or determine the cause of its diversion from its flight plan.

The inability to find flight MH370 after an intensive three-year international search, and an additional three-month search by a private company is conclusive evidence a large commercial airliner can crash into the ocean and not just its location can remain undetected, but the reasons for it going off-course can be unknown.

The vanishing of Malaysian Flight 370 is the world's second greatest aviation mystery.

The greatest mystery is what happened to American Airlines Flight 77 on September 11, 2001. Inexplicable aspects of the "official account" of Flight 77 are explained in Chapter XI – The True Terrorism of September 11, 2001, and in Chapter XVI – The War On Terror Was Triggered By 9/11 Events That Remain Mysterious.

---

[1] What happened to flight MH370, what's the latest news on the Malaysia Airlines plane and is the search still going?, By Amanda Devlin, *The Sun* (London, UK), April 18, 2018, https://www.thesun.co.uk/news/2100795/flight-mh370-malaysia-airlines-latest-news-search/

[2] 4-year-search for missing MH370 plane officially ends: Will the mystery ever be solved?, By Katie Dangerfield, Global News Canada, https://globalnews.ca/news/4238848/missing-malaysia-airlines-flight-mh370-search-ends/

[3] Joint Agency Coordination Centre, Wikipedia: The Free Encyclopedia, https://en.wikipedia.org/wiki/Joint_Agency_Coordination_Centre (last viewed Aug. 1, 2018)

[4] MH370 Safety Investigation Report, July 2, 2018, p. 21, MH370 Official Site, http://mh370.gov.my/en/ (last viewed Aug. 1, 2018)

[5] "Plane parts found on island of Reunion on east coast of Africa near Madagascar but is it MH370?," AAP, AFP and Network Writers, news.com.au, July 30, 2015, https://www.news.com.au/travel/travel-updates/incidents/plane-parts-found-on-island-of-reunion-on-east-coast-of-africa-near-madagascar-but-is-it-mh370/news-story/7d7dc102462fa3253f838b702810c1fb (last viewed Aug. 1, 2018)

[6] "MH370 Was 'Manipulated' Off Course to Its End, Report Says," By Angus Whitley and Pooi Koon Chong , *Bloomberg.com*, July 29, 2018, https://www.bloomberg.com/news/articles/2018-07-30/mh370-investigation-unable-to-determine-cause-of-disappearance (last viewed Aug. 1, 2018)

[7] "MH370 Joint Communique," JACC (Australian Govt.), January 17, 2017, http://jacc.gov.au/media/communiques/2017/com005.aspx (last viewed Aug. 1, 2018)

[8] "Malaysia to pay U.S. firm up to $70 million if it finds missing MH370," *Reuters.com*, January 10, 2018, https://www.reuters.com/article/us-malaysia-airlines-mh370/malaysia-to-pay-u-s-firm-up-to-70-million-if-it-finds-missing-mh370-idUSKBN1EZ0OA (last viewed Aug. 1, 2018)

[9] 4-year-search for missing MH370 plane officially ends: Will the mystery ever be solved?, By Katie Dangerfield, Global News Canada, https://globalnews.ca/news/4238848/missing-malaysia-airlines-flight-mh370-search-ends/ (last viewed Aug. 1, 2018)

[10] MH370 Safety Investigation Report, July 2, 2018, MH370 Official Site, http://mh370.gov.my/en/ (last viewed Aug. 1, 2018)

[11] *Id.* at xiv.

[12] *Id.* at 443.

XVI

The War On Terror Was Triggered By 9/11 Events That Remain Mysterious

What happened on September 11, 2001 remains mysterious because of a multitude of unanswered questions and an official narrative that doesn't comport with reality. (See Chapter XI – The True Terrorism Of September 11, 2001.)

That mystery remains an important issue because those events were the justification for the U.S. launching the War on Terror against alleged foreign terrorists. As a consequence the U.S. military invaded Afghanistan and Iraq – where the U.S. remains involved – and the U.S. is not only involved in other conflicts in the Middle East, but it has expanded its military activities in Africa.

Books and articles have been written detailing the *9/11 Commission Report* issued on July 22, 2004 has more holes than Swiss Cheese in its explanation of what happened regarding the four airliners and the events concerning them in New York, Pennsylvania, and Washington D.C.[1]

Prior to 9/11 no high rise office building in the world had simply fallen down from a non-natural event or fire – and none has fallen down since.[2]

Entire websites are devoted to debunking the 9/11 Commission Report. Esteemed engineers and even physicists have become involved in questioning the official narrative of how the 110 story Twin Towers and the 47 story Building 7 – which wasn't even hit by an airliner – fell down.

Enormous investigative resources have been devoted to exposing the inadequacy of the official explanation regarding why the Twin Towers and WTC Building 7 fell down. Building 7 was 370 feet south of the Twin Towers and fell down about seven hours after they did.[3] A person who didn't know they were watching a video of Building 7 falling down would think they were watching the controlled demotion of the building. That simple fact has not been reasonably explained.

In contrast with the events in New York City, there has been less investigation of the even more mysterious official story of Flight 77 that allegedly struck the Pentagon.

Eyewitness saw each Twin Tower struck by an airliner, and photos and video document that in fact happened. The Pentagon is the headquarters of the U.S. military blanketed by surveillance cameras, and it is not only in a highly populated area, but mid-morning on 9/11 traffic was backed up in front of the Pentagon. Yet there is not a single photograph or video of Flight 77 approaching or striking the Pentagon that is in the public domain. If such a privately taken photo or video exists there is no rational reason why it wouldn't be released. However, if the government is in possession of photos or video disproving Flight 77 caused the Pentagon's damage then there would be great pressure to avoid its public release. Such evidence would destroy the official narrative of what caused the Pentagon's damage on 9/11.

The accounts of people who claim they witnessed what they thought was a commercial airliner approach or strike the Pentagon vary wildly in their details. Other eyewitnesses unequivocally state it wasn't an airliner. Lon Rains, the editor of *Space News*, was stuck in traffic in front of the Pentagon and he stated: "I was convinced it was a missile. It came in so fast it sounded nothing like an airplane."[4] Tom Seibert stated: "We heard what sounded like a missile, then we heard a loud boom."[5]

There were a variety of speculations by government officials about what caused the explosion at the Pentagon until the official story was settled on that the building was struck by Flight 77.

The primary documentary support for the claim that a plane hit the Pentagon is the Flight Data Recorder (FDR) information that was only released in response to a Freedom of Information Act request.

One problem is the alleged Flight 77 FDR data doesn't comport with the reality of the damage to the Pentagon.[6] There are also questions about whether it comports with the flight capabilities of a Boeing 757-200.[7] There are also

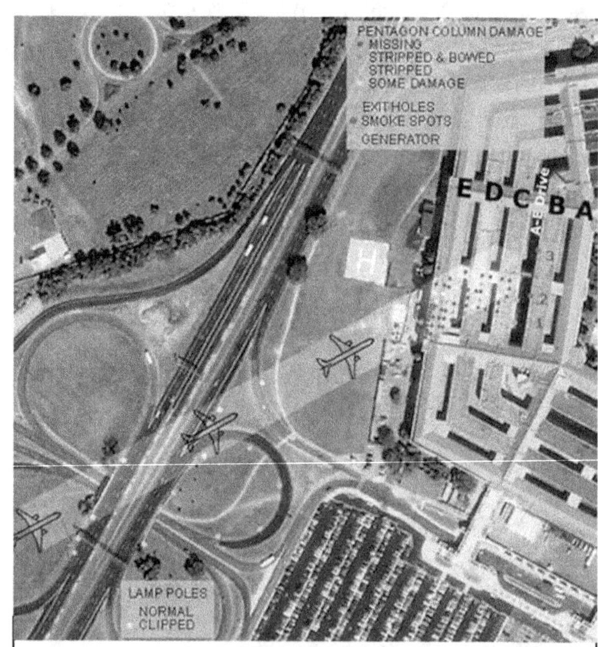

Flight 77's approach to the Pentagon at 61.2 degrees based on Flight Data Recorder analysis, and damage to interior steel columns and exit points. (aerospaceweb.org)

claims the FDR information is not for a 757-200 aircraft.[8]

The purported flight data shows that the airliner was approaching the Pentagon at a descent angle of 5 degrees, at an angle of 61.2 degrees in relation to the front of the building, its wings were banked 0 degrees, the engines were inches above the ground close to the building (there was no damage to the grass),[9] and it was going 483 knots (556 mph) (815 fps) when it struck the building.

The overlay to the right showing the approach based on the Flight Data Recorder and the interior damage raises several obvious questions, and probably many that aren't so obvious. Some of those questions are:

• With the engines inches above the grass why didn't the large generator (that was 8 feet or so high) knock off the right engine and the right wing, or sustain damage from being struck by an object going 556 mph?

• How were the large spools of wire many feet high that were in the flight path untouched?

• How were numerous interior steel and concrete load bearing columns *missing* that were outside the plane's wing span?

• How could photos of the Pentagon's exterior show shredded vertical steel columns bent *outwards* if the damage was caused from the effect of the building being struck by a 757?

• How could two of the three exit holes through the concrete wall into A-E Drive be well outside the plane's wing span?

• How could a 757's fragile airframe have crashed through the E, D, and C Rings – that were filled with interior walls and steel load bearing columns – intact enough to create an approximately 12' circular exit hole, yet leave absolutely no trace of its fuselage, wings, tail, or interior debris?

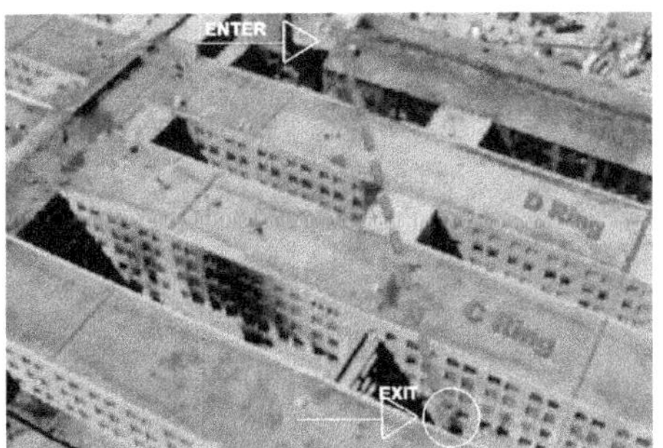

Path through Rings E, D & C of object
that struck the Pentagon
(bibliotecapleyades.net).

A photo of the primary exit hole from Ring C shows it is circular about 12" in diameter.

Pentagon 'C' Ring final punch out hole (bibliotecapleyades.net)

Outside debris left from the making of the Pentagon 'C' Ring punch out hole (citizeninvestigationteam.com).

The debris outside and inside the Pentagon, the physical damage to the building, and other factors, are inconsistent with the impact of a Boeing 757 on the first floor.[10] The above left photo shows there was so little debris you can see all the way through the building to the Pentagon's outside windows.

A simulation by Purdue University's Computing Research Institute purported to show how Flight 77 could have caused the Pentagon's interior structural column damage.[11] However, it completely neglected to address how the _entirety_ of plane's fuselage, wings, tail, and fuel penetrated the building's outer wall structure. Inexplicably, the simulation has the plane approaching the Pentagon and then directly striking its interior steel load bearing columns _on the first floor_ without having to first penetrate the outer wall that at its strongest points was _23" thick_ – 5" of limestone, 8" of brick, and 10" of reinforced concrete.[12] The simulation shows all damage to the planes fuselage and wings as caused from the steel structural columns.

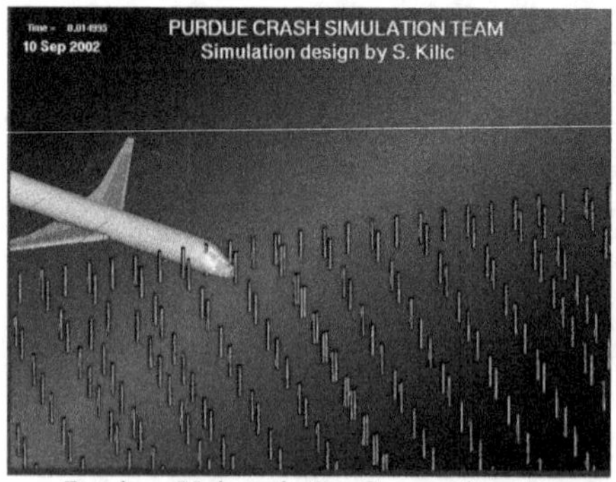

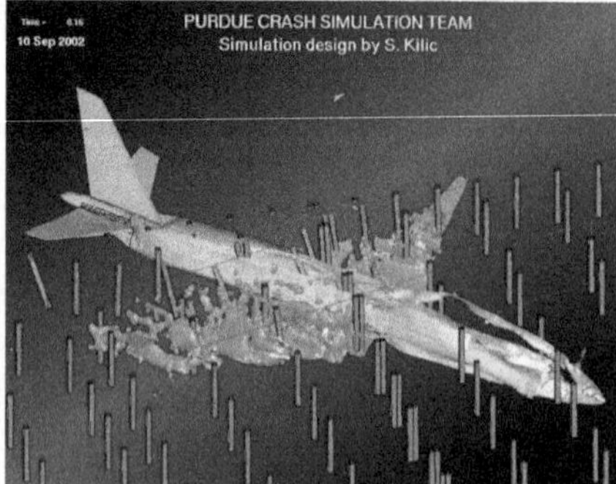

Purdue University's Computing Research Institute Flight 77 simulations regarding interior structural damage.

Another issue that is ignored is the amount of a blow the fuselage of a 757 can withstand without damage – and what happens when that is exceeded.[13] The exterior structure of modern airliners is relatively fragile to impact damage. For example, the carbon nose cone of a Boeing 757-200 carrying the Oklahoma City Thunder basketball team was fractured and caved in by a bird strike during its landing approach in Chicago.[14] Hitting a building with an outer layer of limestone 5" thick and inner layers would be expected to cause immediate catastrophic damage.

Bird strike damage to Boeing 757-200 as Delta Flight dl8935 carry the Oklahoma City Thunder basketball team approached Chicago (MDW). (Steven Adams)

Consequently, a much more interesting and instructive simulation by Purdue's CRI would have been the damage to a B-757 from crashing into the Pentagon's outside wall. Would there have been enough of the plane's structure intact to have penetrated into the buildings interior and cause significant damage? Another simulation would have been what could have happened to the fuel Flight 77 would have had onboard at the time of the explosion at the Pentagon. It had around 11,000 gallons when it took off.[15] The Fire Marshall acknowledged there was no evidence of any of jet fuel at the Pentagon, and he only saw a "small puddle" of a liquid he couldn't readily identify.[16]

A free-lance reporter who filmed the scene at the Pentagon immediately after the incident described the diameter of the whole in the building as no more than the size of a garage door, and there was no damage whatsoever to the grass immediately in front of where the building was struck.[17]

The single most puzzling question is where is the wreckage of Flight 77 if it struck the Pentagon? The following photo was taken minutes after the event occurred, and from left of center it shows the circular hole where some sort of impact or explosion occurred that caused penetration of the Pentagon's outer wall. But there is nothing that even resembles wreckage from an airliner 155' long, with a 124' wingspan and weighing over 200,000 pounds, and there are no bodies.

Pentagon point of impact minutes after explosion (publicintelligence.net)

Compare the absence of aircraft debris at the Pentagon with the plethora of debris visible in the following photos of airliner crash sites around the world.

Concorde Air France Flight 4590 crashed into the 45-room Hotel L'issimo in Gonesse, France on July 25, 2000. All 113 on board died.

Concorde debris after crashing into Hotel L'issimo in Gonesse, France on July 25, 2000 (1001crash.com).

Concorde debris after crashing into Hotel L'issimo in Gonesse, France on July 25, 2000 (1001crash.com).

Concorde debris after crashing into Hotel L'issimo in Gonesse, France on July 25, 2000 (independent.ie).

Boeing 707 BOAC Flight 911 crashed near Mt. Fuji, Japan on March 5, 1966. All 124 on board died.

Avro RJ85 LaMia Flight 2933 crashed into a mountain near Rionegro, Colombia on November 28, 2016. 71 of the 77 on board died.

DC-8 United Airlines Flight 826 had mid-air collision with TWA Constellation over New York City on December 16, 1960. 83 of the 84 people aboard died in the crash, with the one survivor dying the next day. The DC-8 crashed in NYC's Park Slope area, and the Constellation crashed on Staten Island with all 44 aboard dying.

DC-8 United Airlines Flight 826 crashed in a New York City street after mid-air collision with another airliner on December 16, 1960.

Airliners leave evidence, and a lot of it, when they crash. This author has not found a single airliner crash in history in which the crash site didn't contain physical identifiable wreckage. If that was the case with American Airlines Flight 77 on September 11, 2001, then it would be the first known time in history.

As set forth in Chapter XI and above, the most reasonable explanation for the lack of physical evidence Flight 77 crashed into the Pentagon is because it didn't. Given the type of damage to the Pentagon, it would be more fruitful to consider it was most likely struck by a missile, and then less likely by a drone or small jet. (See Chapter XI)

Flight 77 took off from Dulles International Airport at 8:20 a.m. on September 11 bound for Los Angeles. If it didn't hit the Pentagon what happened to it? There has been considerable private investigation, and even a video made, reporting eyewitness accounts that an airliner was seen flying low over Arlington, Virginia before the Pentagon explosion on 9/11, and then flying away.[18]

The evidence available 17 years after the events of 9/11 supports what this author suggested in 2002 is the most logical explanation for what happened to Flight 77:

> The government's manufactured cover story that Flight 77 crashed into the Pentagon is facially absurd. Of course, the great mystery of Flight 77 is where it crashed. It is reasonable to surmise it crashed into the Atlantic Ocean, since its wreckage would have otherwise been found by now if it had crashed on the mainland U.S.[19]

This author appeared on a radio program in 2002 and talked about the only logical explanation for what happened to Flight 77 is it crashed in the Atlantic Ocean. Callers-in pooh-poohed the idea, that may have seemed fantastic at the time.

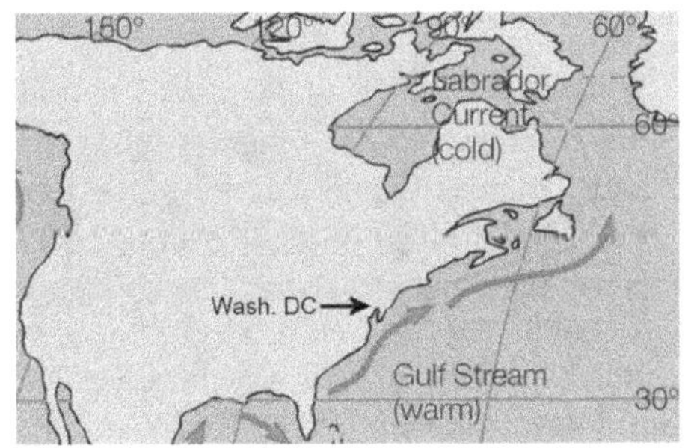

The disappearance of Malaysian Flight 370 on March 8, 2014 and the inability to find its wreckage after the most intensive search in history proves it is entirely realistic. Since no search was conducted for Flight 77, it wouldn't be expected that its light weight surface debris would have been found. Particularly since the Gulf Stream off the east coast flows north into the Arctic Ocean.

If that is the case, then physical evidence of Flight 77 lies somewhere off the east coast in the Atlantic Ocean, and it is possible that some of its surface debris is in the Arctic.

Illusionist David Copperfield had television specials in which he appeared to make large objects disappear. Those "disappeared" objects included a locomotive, the Statute of Liberty, and an airplane.[20] An illusionist works their "magic" by misdirecting the attention of their audience.

There is ample evidence the world's attention was misdirected by the official claim Flight 77 crashed in the Pentagon. The simple question challenging that narrative is: Where is the clear and convincing evidence?

The mass of unanswered questions regarding the fate of Flight 77 makes it the greatest mystery in aviation history.

---

[1] "Final Report of the National Commission on Terrorist Attacks Upon the United States," https://www.govinfo.gov/features/911-commission-report (last viewed Aug. 1, 2018)

[2] The National Institute of Standards and Technology (NIST) conducted a study on the collapse of the 47-story World Trade Center Building 7. On August 21, 2008 NIST lead investigator Shyam Sunder gave a Press Briefing about the findings of the study. He stated "WTC 7 collapsed because of fires fueled by office furnishings." Sunder acknowledged, "This is the first time that we are aware of, that a building taller than about 15 stories has collapsed primarily due to fires." See, Opening Statement, Press Briefing—August 21, 2008, Report on the Collapse of World Trade Center Building 7, online at, https://www.nist.gov/document/remarkssunderaug212008briefingpdf (last viewed Aug. 1, 2018).

[3] Final Report on the Collapse of World Trade Center Building 7, National Institute of Standards and Technology, U.S. Dept. of Commerce, NIST NCSTAR 1A, November 2008, online at, http://ws680.nist.gov/publication/get_pdf.cfm?pub_id=861610 (last viewed Aug. 1, 2018).

[4] "Eyewitness: The Pentagon," by Lon Rains, Editor, *Space News*

[5] "'Everyone was screaming, crying, running. It's like a war zone'," by Julian Borger, Duncan Campbell, Charlie Porter and Stuart Millar, *The Guardian*, 9/12/01

[6] "9/11 Painful Deceptions" is a documentary produced in 2005 that details that the scene at the Pentagon did not match being struck by a Boeing 757. See, "9/11 Painful Deceptions - 2005 (full length)," Uploaded to YouTube.com by Ahijab on September 9, 2012. Online at, https://www.youtube.com/watch?v=ZqrWMCSAPZQ (last viewed September 9, 2018).

See also, Missle Damage to Pentagon: Unseen Pentagon Fraud Footage?. Online at, https://www.bibliotecapleyades.net/sociopolitica/esp_sociopol_911_90.htm (last viewed September 9, 2018). From 911lies.org website, that as of Sept. 9, 2018 is no longer online.

[7] See e.g., "Pentagon 9/11: Scientific Evidence Proves Official Account of 'Flight 77' Is False: Given the topography, the force generated by the transition of 'Flight 77' from its downward path to level flight would cause the aircraft to crash before striking the Pentagon," By Enver Masud, *The Wisdom Fund*, July 2, 2009 and Updated Sept. 11, 2017, http://www.twf.org/News/Y2009/0702-Flight77.html (last viewed September 9, 2018).

[8] "Overwhelming Evidence Pentagon Aircraft Data Is Not From An American Airlines 757," PilotsFor911Truth.org, March 3, 2011, http://pilotsfor911truth.org/no-hard-evidence-aa77.html (last viewed September 9, 2018).

⁹ "This [left] engine impacted a low retaining wall, clearly establishing its height as within inches of the ground.16 Many people have pointed out that the left engine did not mark the lawn." "Flight AA77 on 9/11: New FDR Analysis Supports the Official Flight Path Leading to Impact with the Pentagon," Frank Legge, (B.Sc.(Hons.), Ph.D.) and Warren Stutt, (B.Sc.(Hons.) Comp. Sci.), January 2011.

¹⁰ "A Comparison of actual and expected wing debris resulting from the impact of a Boeing 757 on the Pentagon building, By A. K. Dewdney and G. W. Longspaugh, Revised Dec 19, 2004, http://physics911.net/missingwings/ (last viewed September 9, 2018).

¹¹ September 11 Pentagon Attack Simulations Using LS-Dyna, Phase I, Completed September 11, 2002, Purdue.edu, https://www.cs.purdue.edu/homes/cmh/simulation/phase1/image1/09sep02slow.gif (last viewed September 9, 2018).

Purdue's simulation website is, https://www.cs.purdue.edu/homes/cmh/simulation/ (last viewed September 9, 2018).

¹² The Outer Wall: How Many Inches Of What? Adam Larson / Caustic Logic The Frustrating Fraud, Updated August 5 2007, http://frustratingfraud.blogspot.com/2007/07/outer-wall-how-many-inches-of-what.html (last viewed September 9, 2018).

¹³ Modern jet aircraft structures must be able to withstand one 1.8 kg (4 lb) collision; the empennage (tail) must withstand one 3.6 kg (8 lb) bird collision. Cockpit windows on jet aircraft must be able to withstand one 1.8 kg (4 lb) bird collision without yielding or spalling.

¹⁴ "Radome of Delta Boeing 757-200 was damaged by birdstrike on final approach to Chicago MDW," By AIRLIVE contributors, Airlive.net, October 28, 2017, http://www.airlive.net/alert-radome-of-delta-boeing-757-200-was-damaged-by-birdstrike-on-final-approach-to-chicago-mdw/ (last viewed September 9, 2018).

¹⁵ Boeing 757-200 Specifications, MvN's Boeing 757 Website, http://www.b757.info/boeing-757-200-specifications/ (last viewed September 9, 2018). The minimum fuel capacity of a B-757-200 is 11,276 U.S. gallons.

¹⁶ *9/11: The Big Lie* at 23. 80,000 pounds of jet fuel is approx. 11,940 gallons.

¹⁷ "9/11 - Did Flight 77 Really Crash into The Pentagon? - 3 Conflicting "Official" Black-Box Animations," Uploaded by NRUN65 on April 29, 2016. Online at, https://www.youtube.com/watch?v=3JK1zTuBTZI (last viewed September 9, 2018). The reporter described the hole as "16' in diameter … 20' tops."

¹⁸ See, National Security Alert: 9/11 Pentagon Attack, http://citizeninvestigationteam.com/evidence (last viewed September 9, 2018).

81 minute video "National Security Alert: 9/11 Pentagon Attack" can be watched online at, https://vimeo.com/4777716 (last viewed September 9, 2018).

¹⁹ See endnote 102, referencing text in Chapter XI – The Terrorism After September 11.

²⁰ 9 of David Copperfield's Most Memorable Illusions, By Suzanne Raga, MentalFloss.com, September 16, 2016, http://mentalfloss.com/article/85895/9-david-copperfields-most-memorable-illusions (last viewed September 9, 2018).

XVII

U.S. Is Enmeshed In Endless War In Afghanistan And The Middle East

The U.S. military invaded Iraq in 2003, following its invasion of Afghanistan in 2001, and the U.S. military is still active in both countries, plus Yemen and Syria.

To ostensibly fight terrorism, the U.S. military led the invasion of Afghanistan on October 7, 2001. The United Kingdom and Canada supported the invasion, which was later supported by NATO.

The invasion occurred after the U.S. refused to provide any evidence to the Taliban in Afghanistan that Osama bin Laden and al-Qaeda were involved in the events of September 11, 2001. The Taliban – which controlled large portions of Afghanistan including the capital Kabul, with the rest of the country controlled by the Northern Alliance – refused to them hand over unless they were provided evidence of their involvement.[1] As stated above in Chapters XIII and XIV, that evidence didn't exist.

While the invasion of Afghanistan was ongoing, on March 20, 2003 the U.S. led an invasion of Iraq that was joined by the United Kingdom, Australia, Spain, and Poland. Within a month the Iraqi government collapsed, and on May 1, 2003 President George Bush announced the end of combat operations.[2]

Saddam Hussein was captured by the U.S. military on December 13, 2003. After a trial by Iraqi authorities In November 2005 Hussein was convicted of crimes against humanity and sentenced to death. He was executed by hanging on December 30, 2006.[3]

There was no suggestion by the Bush administration that Iraq was involved in 9/11. The invasion of Iraq was justified by the administration's assertion the Iraqi government had weapons of mass destruction – even though U.N. weapons inspectors in Iraq maintained their inspections were unable to find that any such weapons existed.[4] Bush's administration also asserted the Iraqi government was seeking to develop nuclear weapons – which claim Secretary of State Colin Powell made in a speech to the U.N. The administration and Powell offered no credible evidence that claim was true – even though the mainstream media reported it as if it was true.

Although the Bush Administration offered only rhetoric that wasn't back up by substantive evidence, that Iraq had weapons of mass destruction and was attempting to build an atomic weapon, only 3% of the media in the U.S. was opposed to the 2003 invasion.[5]

The U.S. media belatedly acknowledge long after the invasion, that it had reported erroneous information that influenced the public to support it. In 2004 *The New York Times* publicly acknowledged a September 8, 2002 article titled "U.S. Says Hussein Intensifies Quest for A-Bomb Parts" – was based on discredited information.[6]

Without Hussein to maintain the peace among Iraq's Muslim factions, the Sunnis, the Shiites, and the Kurds, were free to war with each other. Iraq descended into a Mad Max nightmarish world of indiscriminate killings and bombings. The U.S. military couldn't leave if it wanted to because it was the only thing standing between all-out civil war and a likely break-up of Iraq into separate countries representing the Muslim majority for those areas.

The violence ultimately subsided to the point that the Iraq government was able to maintain a degree of control without direct U.S. military involvement, which ended in 2011. The U.S. maintains a significant military presence in Iraq to provide support for the Iraqi government, with no end in sight.

The military's direct involvement in Afghanistan is the U.S.' longest war. The U.S. was directly involved in Vietnam for 11 years, while it has been in Afghanistan for going on 17 years with no end in sight.

The U.S.'s efforts in Afghanistan have been a total failure – assuming the goal of the invasion was to reduce radical Islamic terrorists and eliminate the Taliban. The Taliban is stronger in August 2018 than any time since it abandoned Kabul in November 2001. An August 18, 2018 article published by *RT.com* stated: "The dramatic, and seemingly unstoppable, surge of Taliban offensives across Afghanistan is proof that the US is fast becoming the latest foreign power to succumb to failure in a land known for being the "graveyard of empires".[7] The U.S. military's main tasks in Afghanistan seem to be to keep the pro-U.S. government in power and to protect the poppy fields from being destroyed by the Taliban.[8]

As of July 27, 2018 there have been 2,414 U.S. military deaths in Afghanistan and 20,320 soldiers have been wounded in action. There have also been 1,720 U.S. civilian contractor fatalities.[9]

As of July 2018 there have been 4,542 U.S. military deaths in Iraq and more than 31,952 soldiers have been wounded in action.[10]

From 2001 to 2017 the U.S. has directly spent a minimum of $1.07 trillion in Afghanistan.[11] That doesn't count additional costs that include interest payments on the borrowed money or the long-term cost of caring for soldiers physically and psychologically injured in the conflict.

From 2003 to 2011 the U.S. directly spent a minimum of $1.06 trillion in

Iraq when direct military involvement officially ended.[12] That doesn't count additional costs that includes the ongoing military expenses since 2011, interest payments on the borrowed money, or the long-term cost of caring for soldiers physically and psychologically injured in the conflict.

The U.S. government is engaged in an endless "war on terror" because to all appearances there is no strategy or intention to win, or otherwise end it. Indicative of that is the U.S. government's years long alliance with al-Qaeda and other Muslim terrorist groups in Libya, Syria, and perhaps other countries. As this is written the U.S. is militarily protecting 20,000 to 40,000 al-Qaeda fighters and other terrorists in Idlib – their last Syrian stronghold – from being obliterated by Syrian government forces supported by Russian military assistance.[13]

The Costs of War project estimates the total cost of the post-9/11 U.S. wars through fiscal year 2018 is $5.6 trillion.[14] There is no end in sight for conflicts that never would have begun without orchestrated campaigns of lies and deception by the federal government.

Too many government agencies and private companies are handsomely profiting from the "war on terror" for it to be given the unceremonious immediate burial it deserves. It fuels an almost uncontrolled orgy of government spending with the bill left to be paid by U.S. taxpayers now and in the future. A more accurate name is the "war on American taxpayers."

---

[1] "Timeline: Taliban in Afghanistan," Aljazeera.com, July 4, 2009, https://www.aljazeera.com/news/asia/2009/03/2009389217640837.html (last viewed Aug. 1, 2018). ("Abdul Salaam Zaeef, the Taliban's ambassador to Pakistan, says that bin Laden would not be given up without evidence linking him to the 9/11 attacks.")

[2] "Bush Says Major Combat in Iraq Over," Washington Bureau, FOX News, May 2, 2003, http://www.foxnews.com/story/2003/05/02/bush-says-major-combat-in-iraq-over.html (last viewed Aug. 1, 2018). The Iraqi invasion was euphemistically called *Operation Iraqi Freedom.*

[3] Saddam Hussein: President of Iraq, By The Editors, *Encyclopaedia Britannica,* https://www.britannica.com/biography/Saddam-Hussein (last viewed Aug. 1, 2018).

[4] "United Nations Weapons Inspectors Report To Security Council On Progress In Disarmament Of Iraq," United Nations, March 7, 2003, https://www.un.org/press/en/2003/sc7682.doc.htm (last viewed Aug. 1, 2018).

"The Director-General of the IAEA, Mr. ElBaradei, reported that, after three months of intrusive inspections, the Agency had found no evidence or plausible indication of the revival of a nuclear weapons programme in Iraq. There was also no indication that Iraq had attempted to import uranium since 1990 or that it had attempted to import aluminum tubes for use in centrifuge enrichment." *Id.*

[5] Percent of Iraq War Media Sources (in the United States), Wikipedia: The Free Encyclopedia, https://en.wikipedia.org/wiki/2003_invasion_of_Iraq#cite_note-243 (last viewed Aug. 1, 2018).

[6] "The Times and Iraq," *The New York Times*, May 26, 2014.

[7] "Trump's sanctions on Iran dig deeper grave for US forces in Afghanistan," By Mustafa Andalib (Reuters), *RT.com*, https://www.rt.com/op-ed/436140-afghanistan-iran-sanctions-taliban/ . (last viewed Aug. 1, 2018).

[8] "The U.S. military has openly said that it is protecting Afghani poppy fields." Reported in "Drug War? American Troops Are Protecting Afghan Opium. U.S. Occupation Leads to All-Time High Heroin Production", By Washington's Blog, GlobalResearch.ca, June 28, 2018, https://www.globalresearch.ca/drug-war-american-troops-are-protecting-afghan-opium-u-s-occupation-leads-to-all-time-high-heroin-production/5358053 (last viewed Aug. 1, 2018).

[9] Deaths documented in: "Afghanistan Coalition Military Fatalities By Year," Operation Enduring Freedom, icasualties.org, http://icasualties.org (last viewed Aug. 1, 2018).
Casualties documented in: "United States military casualties in the War in Afghanistan," Wikipedia: The Free Encyclopedia, https://en.wikipedia.org/wiki/United_States_military_casualties_in_the_War_in_Afghanistan#Casualties_by_month_and_year (last viewed Aug. 1, 2018).

[10] Deaths documented in: "Iraq Coalition Casualties: Fatalities By Year," Operation Iraqi Freedom, icasualties.org, http://icasualties.org/Iraq/ByYear.aspx
Casualties documented in: "Casualties of the Iraq War," Wikipedia: The Free Encyclopedia, https://en.wikipedia.org/wiki/Casualties_of_the_Iraq_War (last viewed Aug. 1, 2018).

[11] "Afghanistan War Cost, Timeline and Economic Impact: The Ongoing Costs of the Afghanistan War," By Kimberly Amadeo, TheBalance.com, July 11, 2018, https://www.thebalance.com/cost-of-afghanistan-war-timeline-economic-impact-4122493 (last viewed Aug. 1, 2018).

[12] "Cost of Iraq War, Timeline and Economic Impact: The Ongoing Costs of the Iraq War," By Kimberly Amadeo, TheBalance.com, June 21, 2018,
https://www.thebalance.com/cost-of-iraq-war-timeline-economic-impact-3306301 (last viewed Aug. 1, 2018).

[13] "Congresswoman Accuses Trump, Pence of Shielding Al-Qaeda in Idlib," *sputniknews.com*, September 14, 2018, https://sputniknews.com/us/201809141068043412-trump-pence-alqaeda-idlib/ (last viewed Sept. 15, 2018). Rep. Tulsi Gabbard (HI-02) stated on the floor of the U.S. House of Representatives: "Two days ago, President Trump and Vice President Pence delivered solemn speeches about the attacks on 9/11, talking about how much they care about the victims of al-Qaeda's attack on our country. But, they are now standing up to protect the 20,000 to 40,000 al-Qaeda and other jihadist forces in Syria, and threatening Russia, Syria, and Iran, with military force if they dare attack these terrorists."

[14] "Cost of War: United States Budgetary Costs of Post-9/11 Wars Through FY2018," By Neta C. Crawford, , Watson Institute International & Public Affairs, November 2017, https://watson.brown.edu/costsofwar/figures/2017/us-budgetary-costs-post-911-wars-through-fy2018-56-trillion (last viewed Aug. 1, 2018).
The Cost of War's webpage is, https://watson.brown.edu/costsofwar/ (last viewed Aug. 1, 2018).

XVIII

Liberty Of Americans Has Been Under Assault Since 9/11

There has been a reduction in liberty for Americans and an escalation in governmental abuses of power under the umbrella of national security that are justified by the events on September 11, 2001.

Liberties have been undermined by:

1. Warrantless Wiretapping — It has been publicly known since December 2005 that the National Security Agency flaunts federal laws and Court precedents by the wholesale tapping the American's telephone calls without any probable cause they are involved in criminal activity, or even attempting to obtain a warrant.[1] The NSA also is provided direct access to the U.S.' telecommunications infrastructure by some of the country's largest telecom companies. The NSA is also using sophisticated "data mining" systems to analyze information about the domestic electronic communications of many millions of Americans.[2]

2. Torture, Kidnapping and Detention — In the wake of 9/11 the federal government asserted the authority to designate anyone, including American citizens, as an "enemy combatants" who is not subject to the same protections as a person charged with a crime. The government has kidnapped, detained and tortured many prisoners under the guise they were an "enemy combatant" in violation of international law. The U.S. also engaged in rendition by secretly kidnapping people and moving them to foreign countries where they were tortured and abused. After 9/11 the CIA began maintaining secret prison camps in foreign countries to conduct operations that may also violate international standards.[3] It is believed the interrogation and "black site" prisons are still used by the U.S.[4]

3. Domestic Surveillance —The privacy of Americans is decreasing by the expansion of electronic data collection, tracking, analysis, mining and storage,. The FBI's Investigative Data Warehouse has significantly more than 600 million records. A surveillance society has been created by new technologies exploited by growing government power, and growing private data collection and analysis.[5]

4. Patriot Act Abuse — At the end of 2005 several provisions of the Patriot Act were set to expire. However, Congress reauthorized the law without repealing or altering offensive provisions related to surveillance; anti-money

laundering; border security; the removal of obstacles to terrorism investigations; information sharing between agencies; terrorism laws; and, intelligence gathering.[6]

5. Government Secrecy — The Freedom of Information Act has been weakened with the increasing denial of requests, increased processing times, and increased fees for information. Among the reasons for non-disclosure has been expansion of a catch-all category "sensitive but unclassified," and sweeping claims of "state secrets" to hinder judicial review of government policies that infringe on civil liberties. During the Bush administration there were suggestions to prosecute journalists under the Espionage Act of 1917 to dampen media exposure of questionable, illegal and unconstitutional government conduct that included maintaining secret CIA prisons abroad and the NSA wiretapping program.[7]

6. Real ID — The Real ID Act of 2005 requires the states to standardize the authentication and issuance procedures of their drivers licenses and link to databases to be shared with federal, state and local government officials in every state. States are required to be compliant with Real ID by October 2018, but a state can request an extension for cause. Non-compliant drivers licenses could prevent a person from boarding an airplane or to enter certain government buildings.[8]

7. No Fly Lists and other travel lists. The federal government established a No-Fly list to keep track of people prohibited from traveling due to being labeled a security risks. It is estimated there are about 50,000 people on the No Fly List, but the government doesn't disclose the exact number.[9] There are other travel lists identifying people for special handling – such as more intensive searching of belongings – and it is estimated there are over 650,000 people on those lists. It is difficult if not impossible to be removed from one of the lists, because there are no formal procedures to do so.[10]

8. Travel & Government Building Searches. Everyone who travels by air or who enters many state and federal government buildings – such as a courthouse – is presumed to be a criminal without any probable cause to believe they are. To proceed a person must either go through a metal detector or full body scanner, or grant permission for a body search.[11]

9. Political Spying — Numerous government agencies that include the FBI and the Department of Defense, have engaged in spying on thousands of innocent Americans who were members of numerous socially active organizations. It has been found through the Freedom of Information Act that the FBI has consistently monitored groups that include the Quakers; People for the Ethical Treatment of Animals; Greenpeace; the Arab American Anti-

Defamation Committee; and, the ACLU.[12]

10. Abuse of Material Witness Statute. The material witness statute allows the government to arrest and detain a person who is a "material witness" or has important information about a crime, to ensure they are available to provide their testimony. In the wake of 9/11 the government arrested and detained a number of people as a material witness in alleged terrorism investigations, even though the government made no effort to obtain their testimony. Some of those people were wrongly jailed as alleged material witnesses for more than six months, and one spent more than a year in custody.[13]

---

[1] "Top Ten Abuses of Power Since 9/11," ACLU.org, https://www.aclu.org/other/top-ten-abuses-power-911 (last viewed September 8, 2018)

[2] *Id.*

[3] *Id.*

[4] "What are 'black sites'? 6 key things to know about the CIA's secret prisons overseas," By Julie Vitkovskaya, The Washington Post, January 25, 2017, https://www.washingtonpost.com/news/checkpoint/wp/2017/01/25/what-are-black-sites-6-key-things-to-know-about-the-cias-secret-prisons-overseas/?noredirect=on&utm_term=.afac6164f6ef (last viewed September 8, 2018)

[5] "Top Ten Abuses of Power Since 9/11," ACLU.org, https://www.aclu.org/other/top-ten-abuses-power-911 (last viewed September 8, 2018).

[6] See, "Patriot Act," Wikipedia.org, https://en.wikipedia.org/wiki/Patriot_Act#Title_IX:_Improved_intelligence (last viewed September 8, 2018)

[7] "Top Ten Abuses of Power Since 9/11," ACLU.org, https://www.aclu.org/other/top-ten-abuses-power-911 (last viewed September 8, 2018)

[8] "Real ID Act," Wikipedia.org, https://en.wikipedia.org/wiki/Real_ID_Act (last viewed September 8, 2018).

[9] "No Fly List, Wikipedia.org, https://en.wikipedia.org/wiki/No_Fly_List (last viewed September 8, 2018).

[10] "Top Ten Abuses of Power Since 9/11," ACLU.org, https://www.aclu.org/other/top-ten-abuses-power-911 (last viewed September 8, 2018)

[11] *Id.*

[12] *Id.*

[13] *Id.*

Appendix A – Operation Northwoods

March 9, 1962

Report By The Department Of Defense And Joint Chiefs Of Staff Representative On The Caribbean Survey Group to the Joint Chiefs Of Staff on CUBA PROJECT (TS)

March 12, 1962

Note By The Secretaries to the Joint Chiefs of Staff on NORTHWOODS

March 13, 1962

Memorandum For The Secretary Of Defense
RE: Justification for US Military Intervention in Cuba

March 14, 1962

A Note by the Secretaries on NORTHWOODS

UNCLASSIFIED.

REPORT BY THE DEPARTMENT OF DEFENSE AND JOINT CHIEFS OF STAFF REPRESENTATIVE ON THE CARIBBEAN SURVEY GROUP

to the

JOINT CHIEFS OF STAFF

on

CUBA PROJECT (TS)

The Chief of Operations, Cuba Project, has requested that he be furnished the views of the Joint Chiefs of Staff on this matter by 13 March 1962.

EXCLUDED FROM GDS

JUSTIFICATION FOR US MILITARY INTERVENTION IN CUBA (TS)

THE PROBLEM

1. As requested[*] by Chief of Operations, Cuba Project, the
Joint Chiefs of Staff are to indicate brief but precise
description of pretexts which they consider would provide
justification for US military intervention in Cuba.

FACTS BEARING ON THE PROBLEM

2. It is recognized that any action which becomes pretext
for US military intervention in Cuba will lead to a political
decision which then would lead to military action.

3. Cognizance has been taken of a suggested course of
action proposed[**] by the US Navy relating to generated
instances in the Guantanamo area.

4. For additional facts see Enclosure B.

DISCUSSION

5. The suggested courses of action appended to Enclosure A
are based on the premise that US military intervention will
result from a period of heightened US-Cuban tensions which
place the United States in the position of suffering justifiable grievances. World opinion, and the United Nations
forum should be favorably affected by developing the international image of the Cuban government as rash and irresponsible,
and as an alarming and unpredictable threat to the peace of
the Western Hemisphere.

6. While the foregoing premise can be utilized at the
present time it will continue to hold good only as long as
there can be reasonable certainty that US military intervention
in Cuba would not directly involve the Soviet Union. There is

---

* Memorandum for General Craig from Chief of Operations,
  Cuba Project, subject: "Operation MONGOOSE", dated
  5 March 1962, on file in General Craig's office.
** Memorandum for the Chairman, Joint Chiefs of Staff, from
   Chief of Naval Operations, subject: "Instances to
   Provoke Military Actions in Cuba (TS)", dated 8 March 1962,
   on file in General Craig's office.

2

as yet no bilateral mutual support agreement binding the USSR
to the defense of Cuba, Cuba has not yet become a member of the
Warsaw Pact, nor have the Soviets established Soviet bases
in Cuba in the pattern of US bases in Western Europe. Therefore,
since time appears to be an important factor in resolution of
the Cuba problem, all projects are suggested within the time
frame of the next few months.

CONCLUSION

7. The suggested courses of action appended to Enclosure A
satisfactorily respond to the statement of the problem. However,
these suggestions should be forwarded as a preliminary submission
suitable for planning purposes, and together with similar inputs
from other agencies, provide a basis for development of a single,
integrated, time-phased plan to focus all efforts on the
objective of justification for US military intervention in Cuba.

RECOMMENDATIONS

8. It is recommended that:

a. Enclosure A together with its attachments should be
forwarded to the Secretary of Defense for approval and
transmittal to the Chief of Operations, Cuba Project.

b. This paper NOT be forwarded to commanders of unified
or specified commands.

c. This paper NOT be forwarded to US officers assigned
to NATO activities.

d. This paper NOT be forwarded to the Chairman, US
Delegation, United Nations Military Staff Committee.

3

MEMORANDUM FOR THE SECRETARY OF DEFENSE

Subject: Justification for US Military Intervention
            in Cuba (TS)

1. The Joint Chiefs of Staff have considered the attached
Memorandum for the Chief of Operations, Cuba Project, which
responds to a request* of that office for brief but precise
description of pretexts which would provide justification
for US military intervention in Cuba.

2. The Joint Chiefs of Staff recommend that the proposed
memorandum be forwarded as a preliminary submission suitable
for planning purposes. It is assumed that there will be
similar submissions from other agencies and that these inputs
will be used as a basis for developing a time-phased plan.
Individual projects can then be considered on a case-by-case
basis.

3. Further, it is assumed that a single agency will be
given the primary responsibility for developing military and
para-military aspects of the basic plan. It is recommended
that this responsibility for both overt and covert military
operations be assigned the Joint Chiefs of Staff.

---

* Memorandum for Gen Craig from Chief of Operations, Cuba
  Project, subject, "Operation MONGOOSE", dated 5 March
  1962, on file in Gen Craig's office

4

Enclosure A

DRAFT

MEMORANDUM FOR CHIEF OF OPERATIONS, CUBA PROJECT

Subject: Justification for US Military Intervention
in Cuba (TS)

1. Reference is made to memorandum from Chief of Operations, Cuba Project, for General Craig, subject: "Operation MONGOOSE" dated 5 March 1962, which requested brief but precise description of pretexts which the Joint Chiefs of Staff consider would provide justification for US military intervention in Cuba.

2. The projects listed in the enclosure hereto are forwarded as a preliminary submission suitable for planning purposes. It is assumed that there will be similar submissions from other agencies and that these inputs will be used as a basis for developing a time-phased plan. The individual projects can then be considered on a case-by-case basis.

3. This plan, incorporating projects selected from the attached suggestions, or from other sources, should be developed to focus all efforts on a specific ultimate objective which would provide adequate justification for US military intervention. Such a plan would enable a logical build-up of incidents to be combined with other seemingly unrelated events to camouflage the ultimate objective and create the necessary impression of Cuban rashness and irresponsibility on a large scale, directed at other countries as well as the United States. The plan would also properly integrate and time phase the courses of action to be pursued. The desired resultant from the execution of this plan would be to place the United States in the apparent position of suffering defensible grievances from a rash and irresponsible government of Cuba and to develop an international image of a Cuban threat to peace in the Western Hemisphere.

4. Time is an important factor in resolution of the Cuban
problem. Therefore, the plan should be so time-phased that
projects would be operable within the next few months.

5. Inasmuch as the ultimate objective is overt military
intervention, it is recommended that primary responsibility
for developing military and para-military aspects of the plan
for both overt and covert military operations be assigned the
Joint Chiefs of Staff.

Appendix to
Enclosure A

6

UNCLASSIFIED

PRETEXTS TO JUSTIFY US MILITARY INTERVENTION IN CUBA

(Note: The courses of action which follow are a preliminary submission suitable only for planning purposes. They are arranged neither chronologically nor in ascending order. Together with similar inputs from other agencies, they are intended to provide a point of departure for the development of a single, integrated, time-phased plan. Such a plan would permit the evaluation of individual projects within the context of cumulative, correlated actions designed to lead inexorably to the objective of adequate justification for US military intervention in Cuba).

1. Since it would seem desirable to use legitimate provocation as the basis for US military intervention in Cuba a cover and deception plan, to include requisite preliminary actions such as has been developed in response to Task 33 c, could be executed as an initial effort to provoke Cuban reactions. Harassment plus deceptive actions to convince the Cubans of imminent invasion would be emphasized. Our military posture throughout execution of the plan will allow a rapid change from exercise to intervention if Cuban response justifies.

2. A series of well coordinated incidents will be planned to take place in and around Guantanamo to give genuine appearance of being done by hostile Cuban forces.

a. Incidents to establish a credible attack (not in chronological order):

(1) Start rumors (many). Use clandestine radio.

(2) Land friendly Cubans in uniform "over-the-fence" to stage attack on base.

(3) Capture Cuban (friendly) saboteurs inside the base.

(4) Start riots near the base main gate (friendly Cubans).

(5) Blow up ammunition inside the base; start fires.

(6) Burn aircraft on air base (sabotage).

(7) Lob mortar shells from outside of base into base. Some damage to installations.

(8) Capture assault teams approaching from the sea or vicinity of Guantanamo City.

(9) Capture militia group which storms the base.

(10) Sabotage ship in harbor; large fires -- napthalene.

(11) Sink ship near harbor entrance. Conduct funerals for mock-victims (may be lieu of (10)).

b. United States would respond by executing offensive operations to secure water and power supplies, destroying artillery and mortar emplacements which threaten the base.

c. Commence large scale United States military operations.

3. A "Remember the Maine" incident could be arranged in several forms:

a. We could blow up a US ship in Guantanamo Bay and blame Cuba.

b. We could blow up a drone (unmanned) vessel anywhere in the Cuban waters. We could arrange to cause such incident in the vicinity of Havana or Santiago as a spectacular result of Cuban attack from the air or sea, or both. The presence of Cuban planes or ships merely investigating the intent of the vessel could be fairly compelling evidence that the ship was taken under attack. The nearness to Havana or Santiago would add credibility especially to those people that might have heard the blast or have seen the fire. The US could follow up with an air/sea rescue operation covered by US fighters to "evacuate" remaining members of the non-existent crew. Casualty lists in US newspapers would cause a helpful wave of national indignation.

4. We could develop a Communist Cuban terror campaign in the Miami area, in other Florida cities and even in Washington.

8

Annex to Appendix
to Enclosure A

The terror campaign could be pointed at Cuban refugees seeking
haven in the United States. We could sink a boatload of Cubans
enroute to Florida (real or simulated). We could foster attempts
on lives of Cuban refugees in the United States even to the
extent of wounding in instances to be widely publicized.
Exploding a few plastic bombs in carefully chosen spots, the
arrest of Cuban agents and the release of prepared documents
substantiating Cuban involvement also would be helpful in
projecting the idea of an irresponsible government.

5. A "Cuban-based, Castro-supported" filibuster could be
simulated against a neighboring Caribbean nation (in the vein
of the 14th of June invasion of the Dominican Republic). We
know that Castro is backing subversive efforts clandestinely
against Haiti, Dominican Republic, Guatemala, and Nicaragua at
present and possible others. These efforts can be magnified and
additional ones contrived for exposure. For example, advantage
can be taken of the sensitivity of the Dominican Air Force to
intrusions within their national air space. "Cuban" B-26 or
C-46 type aircraft could make cane-burning raids at night.
Soviet Bloc incendiaries could be found. This could be coupled
with "Cuban" messages to the Communist underground in the
Dominican Republic and "Cuban" shipments of arms which would
be found, or intercepted, on the beach.

6. Use of MIG type aircraft by US pilots could provide
additional provocation. Harassment of civil air, attacks on
surface shipping and destruction of US military drone aircraft
by MIG type planes would be useful as complementary actions.
An F-86 properly painted would convince air passengers that they
saw a Cuban MIG, especially if the pilot of the transport were
to announce such fact. The primary drawback to this suggestion
appears to be the security risk inherent in obtaining or modify-
ing an aircraft. However, reasonable copies of the MIG could
be produced from US resources in about three months.

9

Annex to Appendix
to Enclosure A

7. Hijacking attempts against civil air and surface craft
should appear to continue as harassing measures condoned by the
government of Cuba. Concurrently, genuine defections of Cuban
civil and military air and surface craft should be encouraged.

8. It is possible to create an incident which will demonstrate
convincingly that a Cuban aircraft has attacked and shot down
a chartered civil airliner enroute from the United States to
Jamaica, Guatemala, Panama or Venezuela. The destination would
be chosen only to cause the flight plan route to cross Cuba.
The passengers could be a group of college students off on a
holiday or any grouping of persons with a common interest to
support chartering a non-scheduled flight.

a. An aircraft at Eglin AFB would be painted and
numbered as an exact duplicate for a civil registered
aircraft belonging to a CIA proprietary organization in the
Miami area. At a designated time the duplicate would be
substituted for the actual civil aircraft and would be
loaded with the selected passengers, all boarded under
carefully prepared aliases. The actual registered
aircraft would be converted to a drone.

b. Take off times of the drone aircraft and the actual
aircraft will be scheduled to allow a rendezvous south of
Florida. From the rendezvous point the passenger-carrying
aircraft will descend to minimum altitude and go directly
into an auxiliary field at Eglin AFB where arrangements will
have been made to evacuate the passengers and return the
aircraft to its original status. The drone aircraft
meanwhile will continue to fly the filed flight plan. When
over Cuba the drone will being transmitting on the international distress frequency a "MAY DAY" message stating he
is under attack by Cuban MIG aircraft. The transmission
will be interrupted by destruction of the aircraft which will
be triggered by radio signal. This will allow ICAO radio

Annex to Appendix
to Enclosure A

stations in the Western Hemisphere to tell the US what
has happened to the aircraft instead of the US trying to
"sell" the incident.

9. It is possible to create an incident which will make it
appear that Communist Cuban MIGs have destroyed a USAF aircraft
over international waters in an unprovoked attack.

   a. Approximately 4 or 5 F-101 aircraft will be dispatched
in trail from Homestead AFB, Florida, to the vicinity of Cuba.
Their mission will be to reverse course and simulate fakir
aircraft for an air defense exercise in southern Florida.
These aircraft would conduct variations of these flights at
frequent intervals. Crews would be briefed to remain at
least 12 miles off the Cuban coast; however, they would be
required to carry live ammunition in the event that hostile
actions were taken by the Cuban MIGs.

   b. On one such flight, a pre-briefed pilot would fly
tail-end Charley at considerable interval between aircraft.
While near the Cuban Island this pilot would broadcast that
he had been jumped by MIGs and was going down. No other
calls would be made. The pilot would then fly directly
west at extremely low altitude and land at a secure base, an
Eglin auxiliary. The aircraft would be met by the proper
people, quickly stored and given a new tail number. The
pilot who had performed the mission under an alias, would
resume his proper identity and return to his normal place
of business. The pilot and aircraft would then have
disappeared.

   c. At precisely the same time that the aircraft was
presumably shot down a submarine or small surface craft
would disburse F-101 parts, parachute, etc., at approximately
15 to 20 miles off the Cuban coast and depart. The pilots
returning to Homestead would have a true story as far as
they knew. Search ships and aircraft could be dispatched
and parts of aircraft found.

Annex to Appendix
to Enclosure A

FACTS BEARING ON THE PROBLEM

1. The Joint Chiefs of Staff have previously stated[*]
that US unilateral military intervention in Cuba can be
undertaken in the event that the Cuban regime commits hostile
acts against US forces or property which would serve as an
incident upon which to base overt intervention.

2. The need for positive action in the event that current
covert efforts to foster an internal Cuban rebellion are
unsuccessful was indicated[**] by the Joint Chiefs of Staff
on 7 March 1962, as follows:

> " - - - determination that a credible internal
> revolt is impossible of attainment during the next
> 9-10 months will require a decision by the United States
> to develop a Cuban "provocation" as justification for
> positive US military action."

3. It is understood that the Department of State also is
preparing suggested courses of action to develop justification
for US military intervention in Cuba.

---

[*] JCS 1969/303
[**] JCS 1969/313

NOTE BY THE SECRETARIES

to the

JOINT CHIEFS OF STAFF

on

NORTHWOODS (S)

A report* on the above subject is submitted for consideration by the Joint Chiefs of Staff.

F. J. BLOUIN

M. J. INGELIDO

Joint Secretariat

---

* Not reproduced herewith; on file in Joint Secretariat

UNCLASSIFIED

13 March 1962

MEMORANDUM FOR THE SECRETARY OF DEFENSE

Subject: Justification for US Military Intervention
in Cuba (TS)

1. The Joint Chiefs of Staff have considered the attached Memorandum for the Chief of Operations, Cuba Project, which responds to a request of that office for brief but precise description of pretexts which would provide justification for US military intervention in Cuba.

2. The Joint Chiefs of Staff recommend that the proposed memorandum be forwarded as a preliminary submission suitable for planning purposes. It is assumed that there will be similar submissions from other agencies and that these inputs will be used as a basis for developing a time-phased plan. Individual projects can then be considered on a case-by-case basis.

3. Further, it is assumed that a single agency will be given the primary responsibility for developing military and para-military aspects of the basic plan. It is recommended that this responsibility for both overt and covert military operations be assigned the Joint Chiefs of Staff.

For the Joint Chiefs of Staff:

L. L. LEMNITZER
Chairman
Joint Chiefs of Staff

SYSTEMATICALLY REVIEWED
BY JCS ON ___________
CLASSIFICATION CONTINUED

1 Enclosure
Memo for Chief of Operations, Cuba Project

EXCLUDED FROM C

JCS 1969/321
14 March 1962

SPECIAL DISTRIBUTION

JOINT CHIEFS OF STAFF

DECISION ON JCS 1969/321

A Note by the Secretaries

on

NORTHWOODS (S)

Note by the Secretaries

1. At their meeting on 13 March 1962, the Joint Chiefs of Staff approved the recommendations in paragraph 8 of JCS 1969/321.

2. In that the Commandant had expressed direct concern of the Marine Corps in this matter, the provisions of Title 10, US Code 141 (c), applied and were followed.

3. This decision now becomes a part of and shall be attached as the top sheet of JCS 1969/321.

F. J. BLOUIN
M. J. INGELIDO
Joint Secretaries

SYSTEMATICALLY REVIEWED
BY JCS ON
CLASSIFICATION CONTINUED

Appendix B – Human Rights Protections In The Soviet Constitution Of 1936

The following articles in Constitution of the USSR (Adopted December 1936) are presented to satisfy the doubts of anyone about the plethora of individual protections specifically enumerated in it. None of these symbolic declaration of rights actually protected anyone from the Soviet Union's federal government when it wanted to exercise its effectively unlimited power, that was no more checked than that of the U.S.'s federal government of today.

Chapter X
Fundamental Rights and Duties of Citizens

Article 118. Citizens of the U.S.S.R. have the *right to work*, that is, are guaranteed the right to employment and payment for their work in accordance with its quantity and quality. …

Article 119. Citizens of the U.S.S.R. have the *right to rest and leisure*. The right to rest and leisure is ensured by the reduction of the working day to seven hours for the overwhelming majority of the workers, the institution of annual vacations with full pay for workers and employees and the provision of a wide network of sanatoria, rest homes and clubs for the accommodation of the working people.

Article 120. Citizens of the U.S.S.R. have the *right to maintenance in old age and also in case of sickness or loss of capacity to work*. This right is ensured by the extensive development of social insurance of workers and employees at state expense, free medical service for the working people and the provision of a wide network of health resorts for the use of the working people.

Article 121. Citizens of the U.S.S.R. have the *right to education*. This right is ensured by universal, compulsory elementary education; by education, including higher education, being free of charge; by the system of state stipends for the overwhelming majority of students in the universities and colleges; by instruction in schools being conducted in the native language, and by the organization in the factories, state farms, machine and tractor stations and collective farms of free vocational, technical and agronomic training for the working people.

Article 122. *Women in the U.S.S.R. are accorded equal rights* with men in all spheres of economic, state, cultural, social and political life. The possibility of exercising these rights is ensured to women by granting them an equal right with men to work, payment for work, rest and leisure, social insurance and education, and by state protection of the interests of mother and child, prematernity and maternity leave with full pay, and the provision of a wide network of maternity homes, nurseries and kindergartens.

Article 123. *Equality of rights of citizens of the U.S.S.R., irrespective of their nationality or race*, in all spheres of economic, state, cultural, social and political life, is an indefeasible law. Any direct or indirect restriction of the rights of, or, conversely, any establishment of direct or indirect privileges for, citizens on account of their race or nationality, as well as any advocacy of racial or national exclusiveness or hatred and contempt, is punishable by law.

Article 124. In order *to ensure to citizens freedom of conscience, the church in the U.S.S.R. is separated from the state*, and the school from the church. Freedom of religious worship and freedom of antireligious propaganda is recognized for all citizens.

Article 125. In conformity with the interests of the working people, and in order to strengthen the socialist system, the *citizens* of the U.S.S.R. *are guaranteed by law*:

freedom of speech;

freedom of the press;

freedom of assembly, including the holding of mass meetings;

freedom of street processions and demonstrations.

These civil rights are ensured by placing at the disposal of the working people and their organizations printing presses, stocks of paper, public buildings, the streets, communications facilities and other material requisites for the exercise of these rights.

Article 126. In conformity with the interests of the working people, and in order to develop the organizational initiative and political activity of the masses of the people, citizens of the U.S.S.R. are ensured the *right to unite in public organizations*--trade unions, cooperative associations, youth organizations,' sport and defense organizations, cultural, technical and scientific societies; and the most active and politically most conscious citizens in the ranks of the working class and other sections of the working people unite in the Communist Party of the Soviet Union (Bolsheviks), which is the vanguard of the working people in their struggle to strengthen and develop the socialist system and is the leading core of all organizations of the working people, both public and state.

Article 127. Citizens of the U.S.S.R. are *guaranteed inviolability of the person. No person may be placed under arrest except by decision of a court or with the sanction of a procurator.*

Article 128. *The inviolability of the homes of citizens and privacy of correspondence are protected by law.*

Article 129. The U.S.S.R. affords the *right of asylum to foreign citizens* persecuted for defending the interests of the working people, or for their scientific activities, or for their struggle for national liberation.

Article 130. It is the duty of every citizen of the U.S.S.R. to abide by the Constitution of the Union of Soviet Socialist Republics, to observe the laws, to maintain labor discipline, honestly to perform public duties, and to respect the rules of socialist intercourse.

The Soviet Constitution of 1936 is available on the Bucknell University website at:
http://www.departments.bucknell.edu/russian/const/36cons04.html#chap10 (last viewed August 28, 2018) (Italics added to original.)

Index

www.ingramcontent.com/pod-product-compliance
Lightning Source LLC
Chambersburg PA
CBHW061816250726
48657CB00001B/461